Introduction

Many people believe that each color goes with a certain Chakra.

Chakras are energy forces linked to our bodies and pur environments and they help with our well-being.

That's why mandalas are so good for your well-being, because they have chakras in them.

In the end, they're a mythical technique that can bring you a lot of different benefits.

« A mandala is the psychological expression of the totality of the self. » -Carl JUNG-

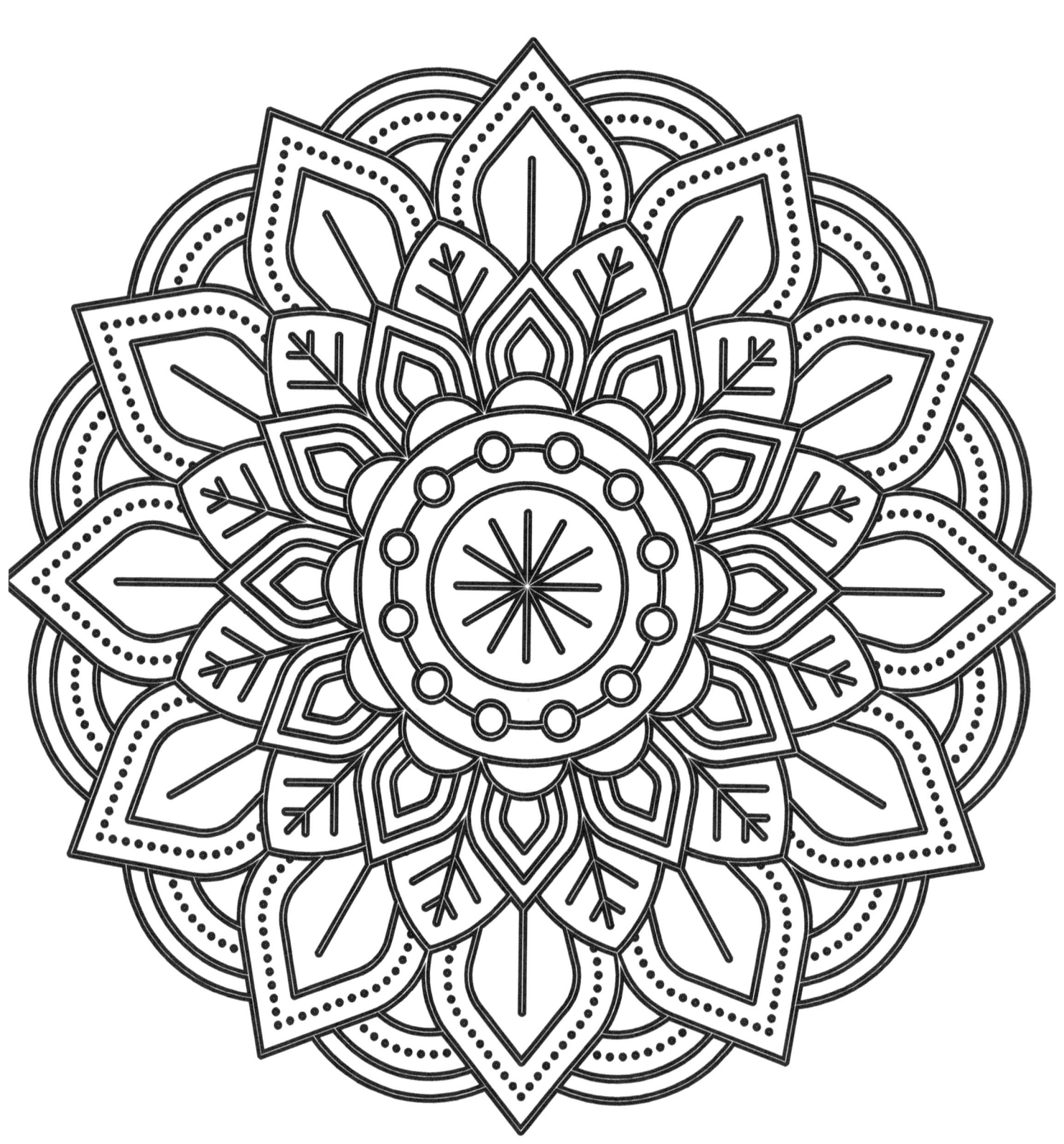

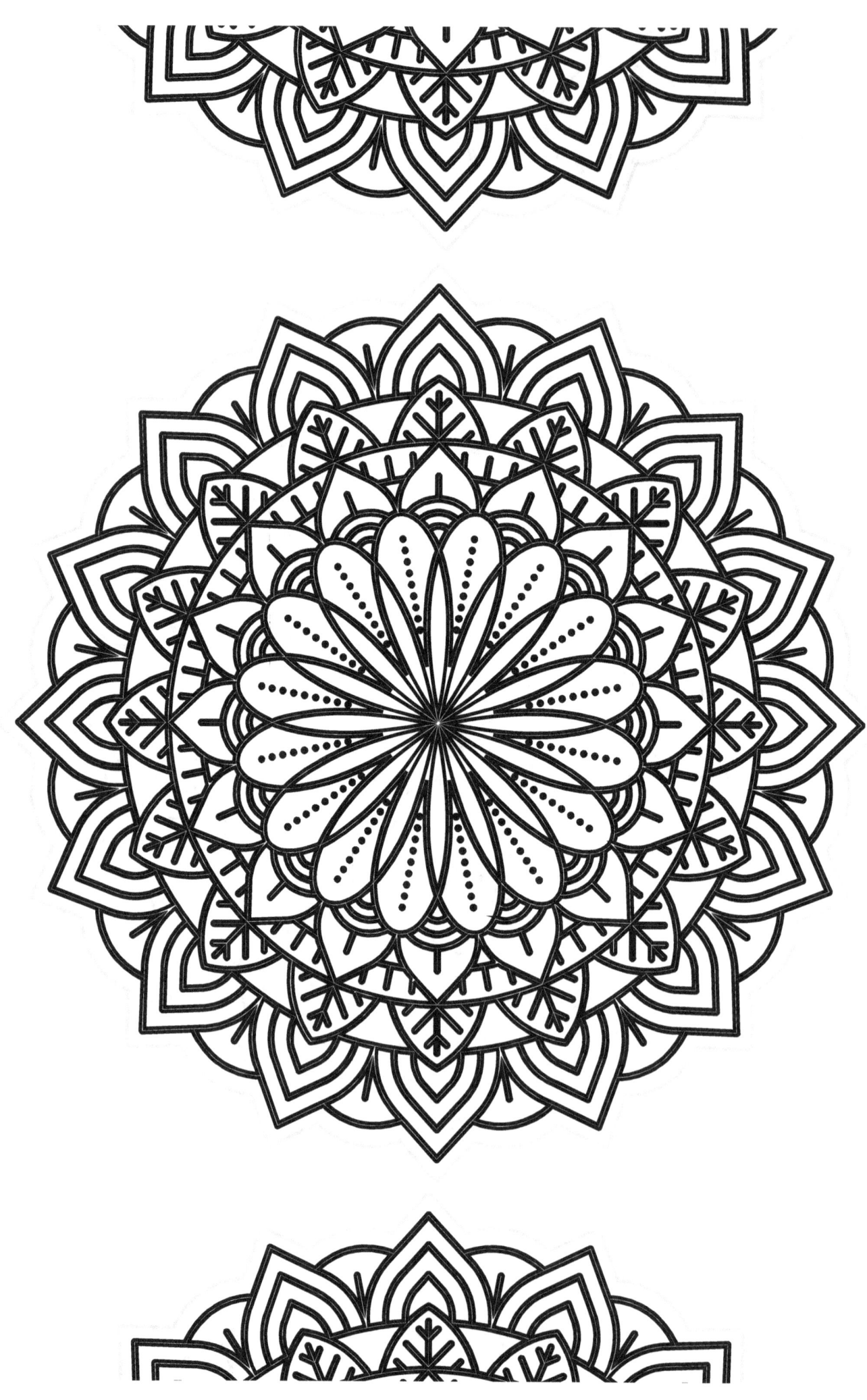

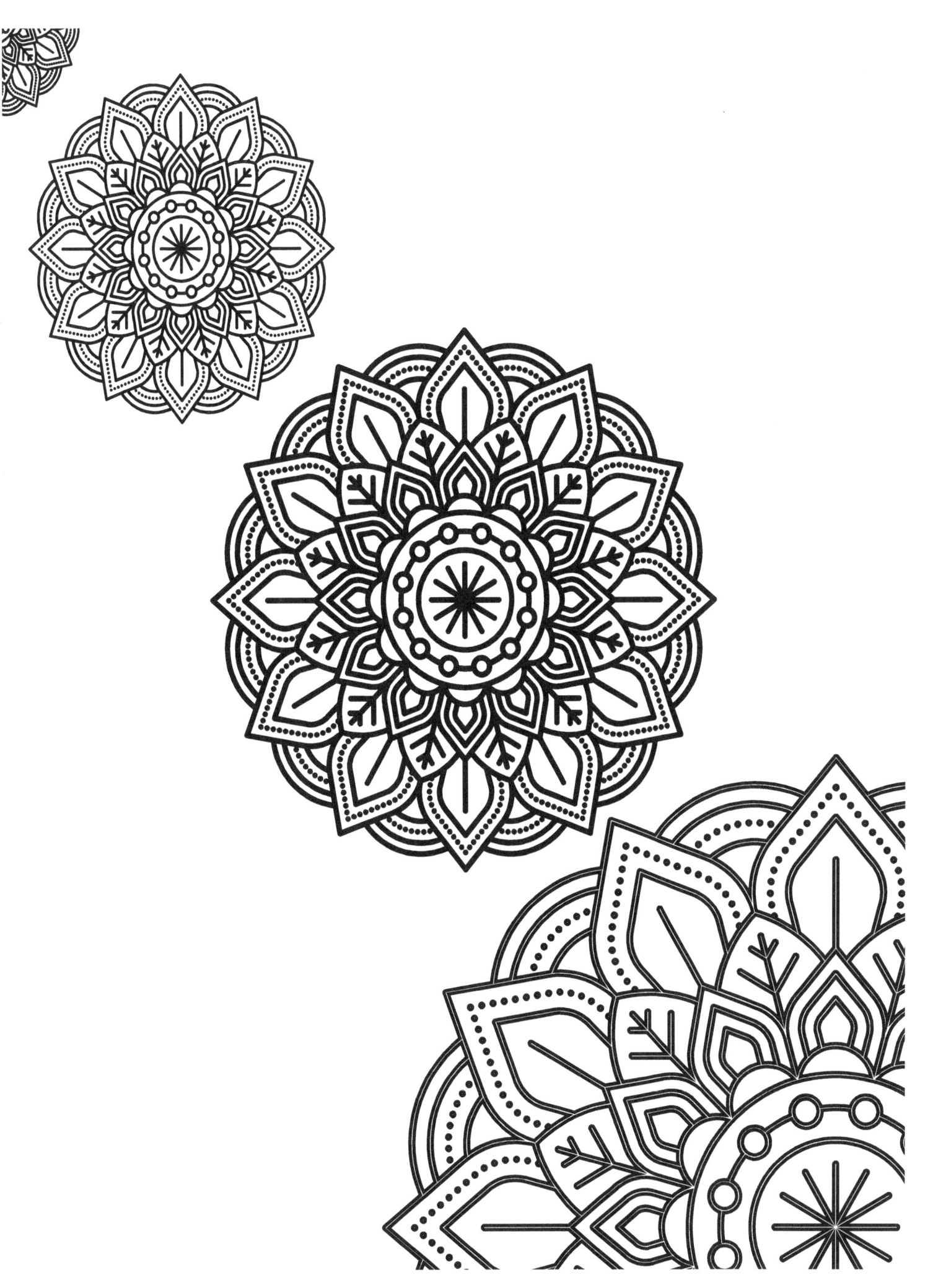

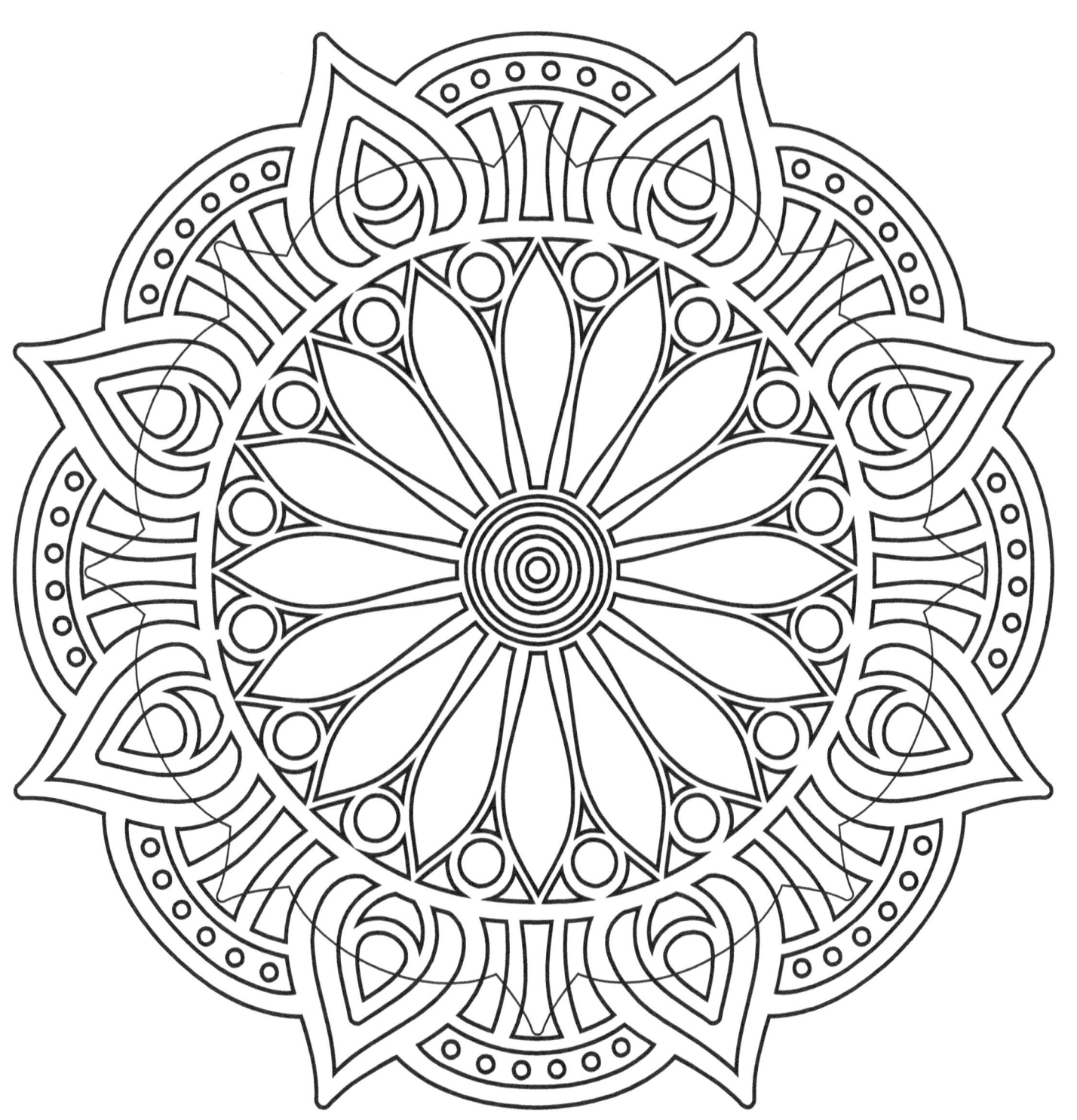

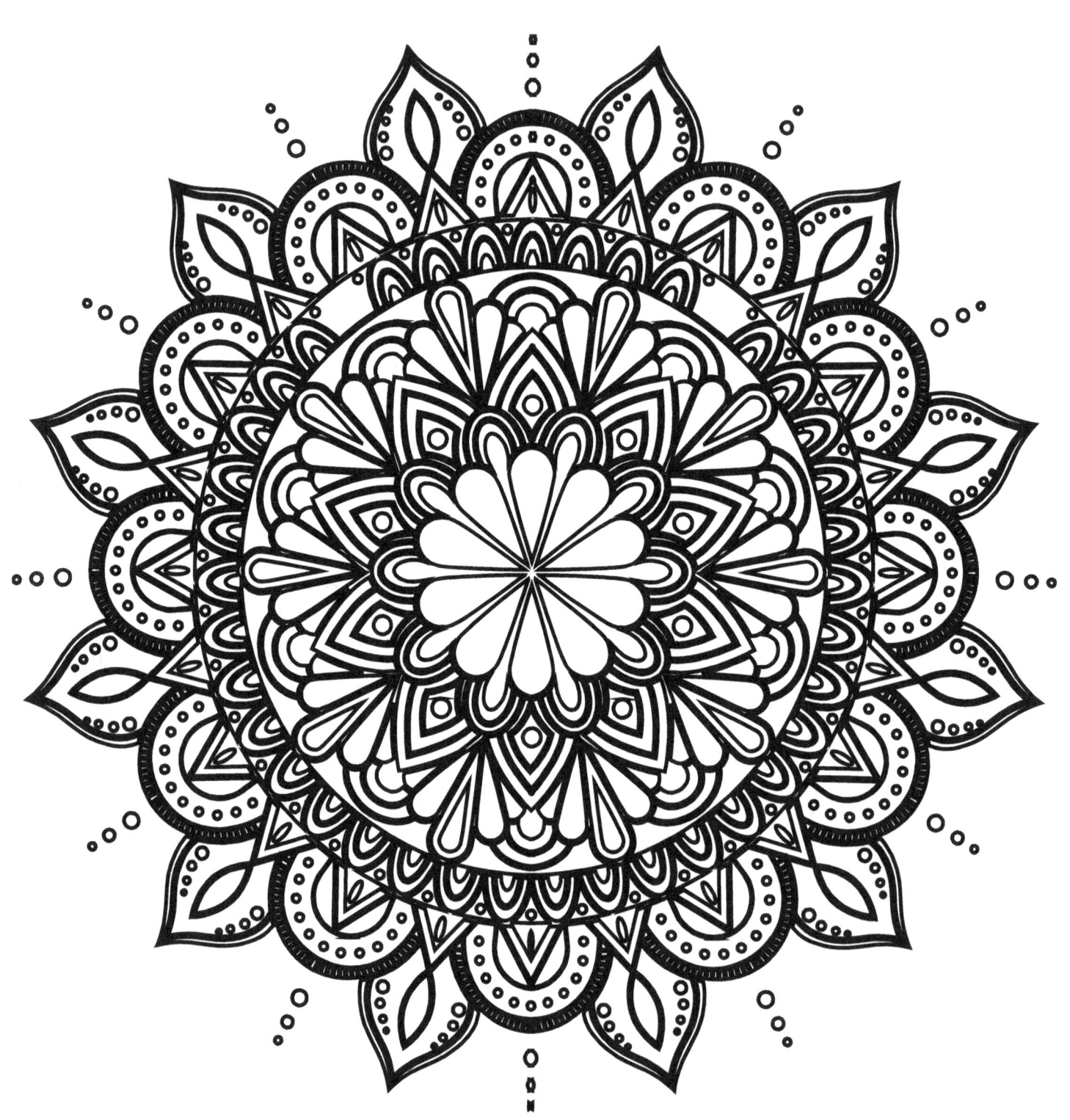

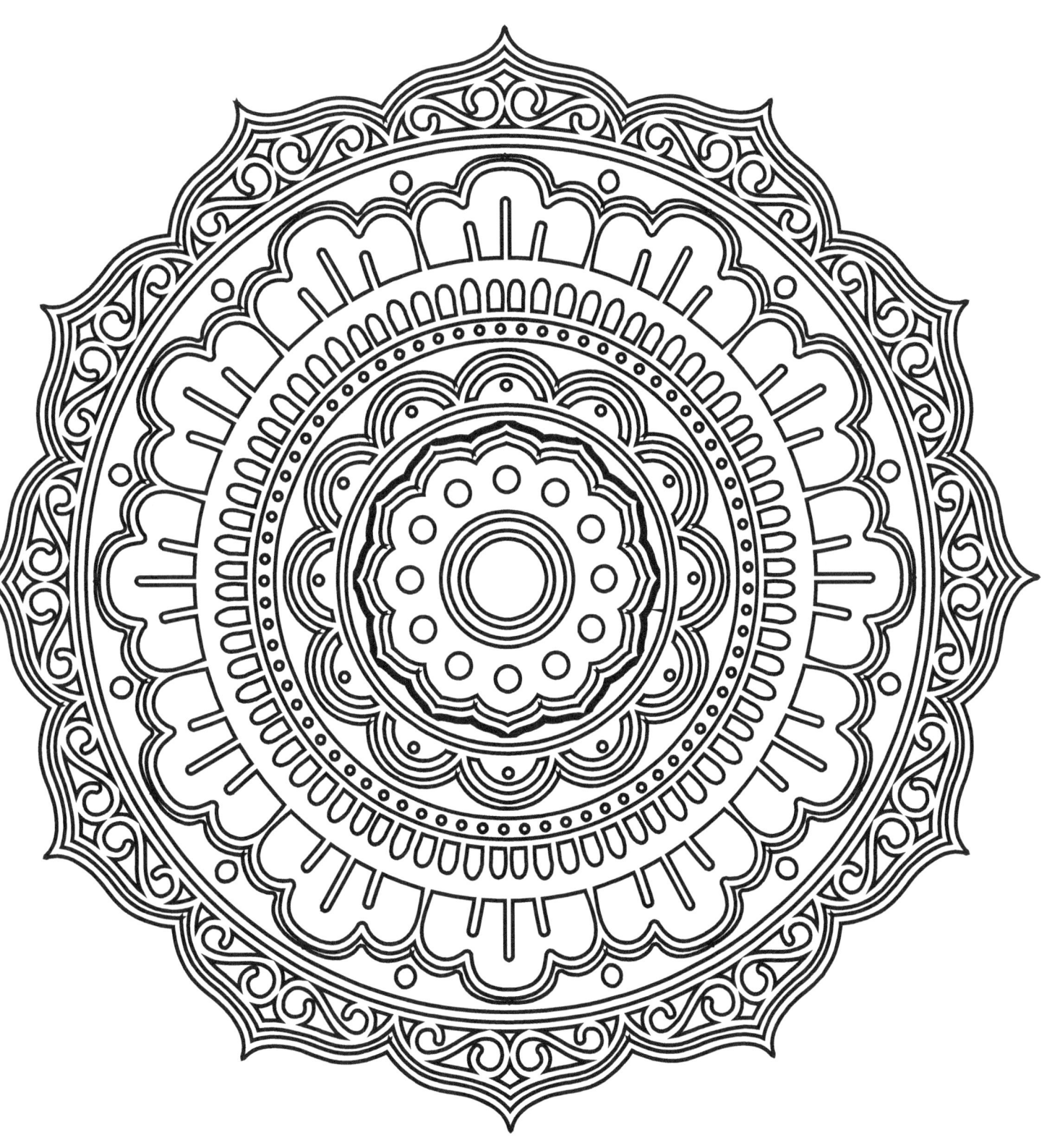

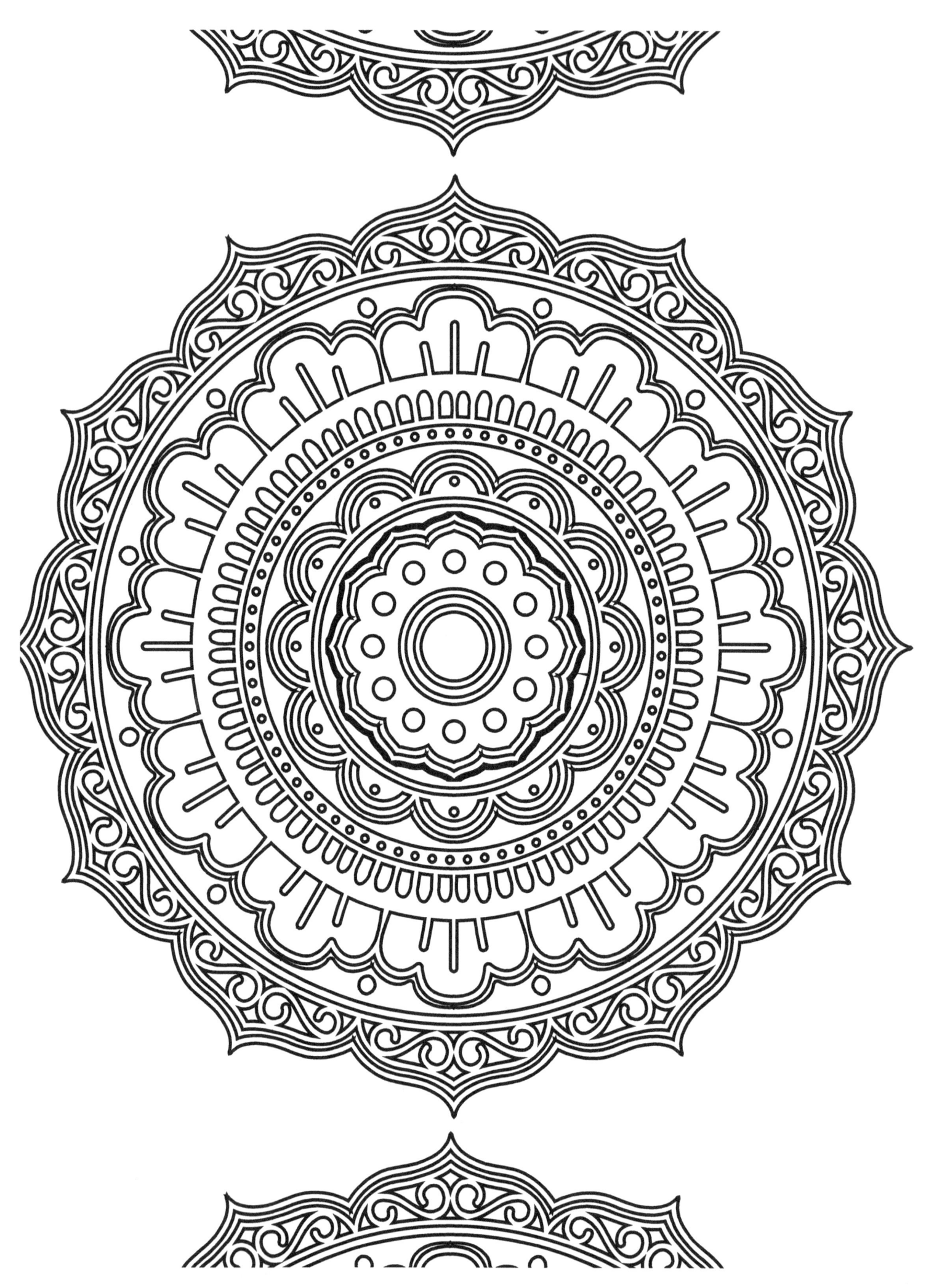

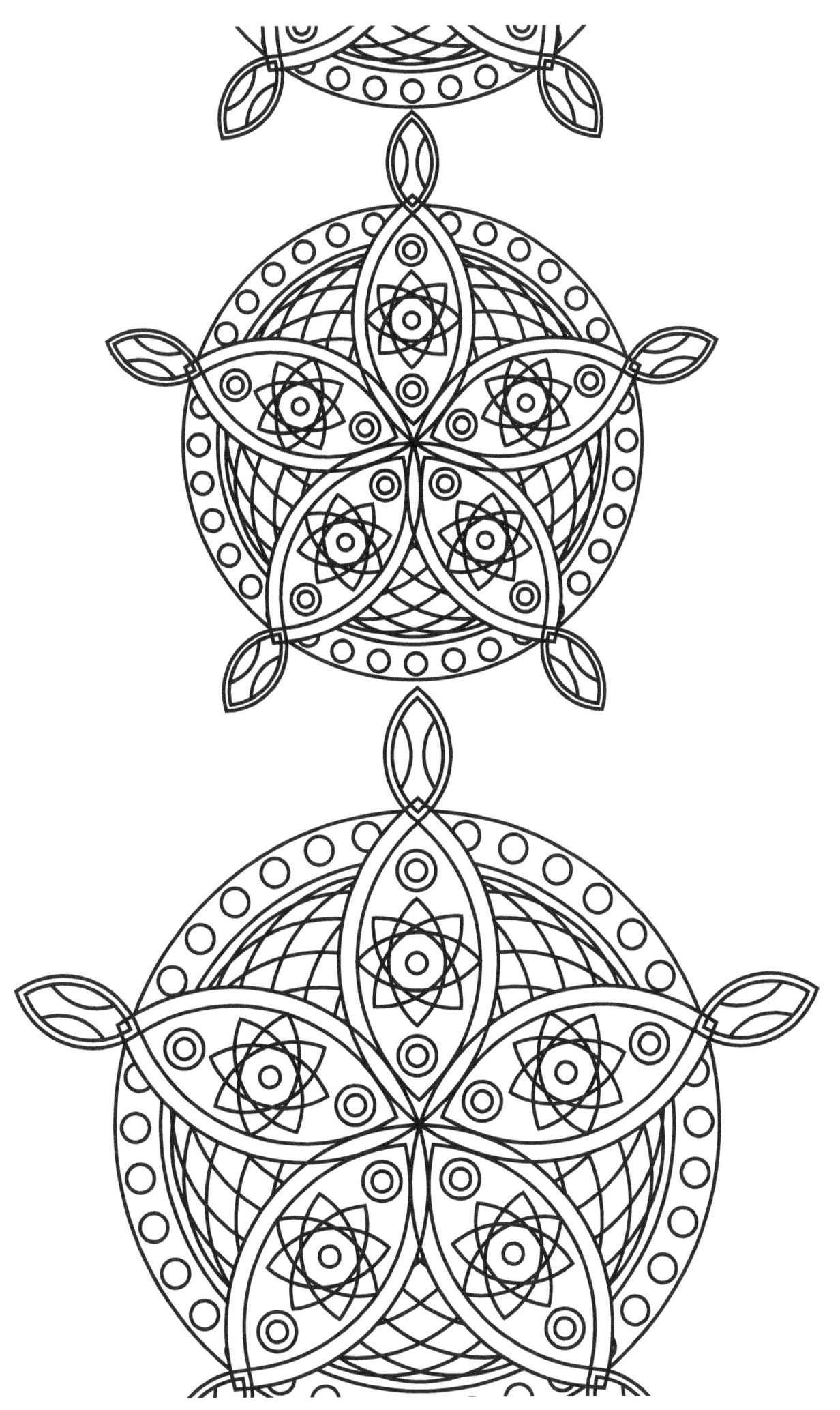

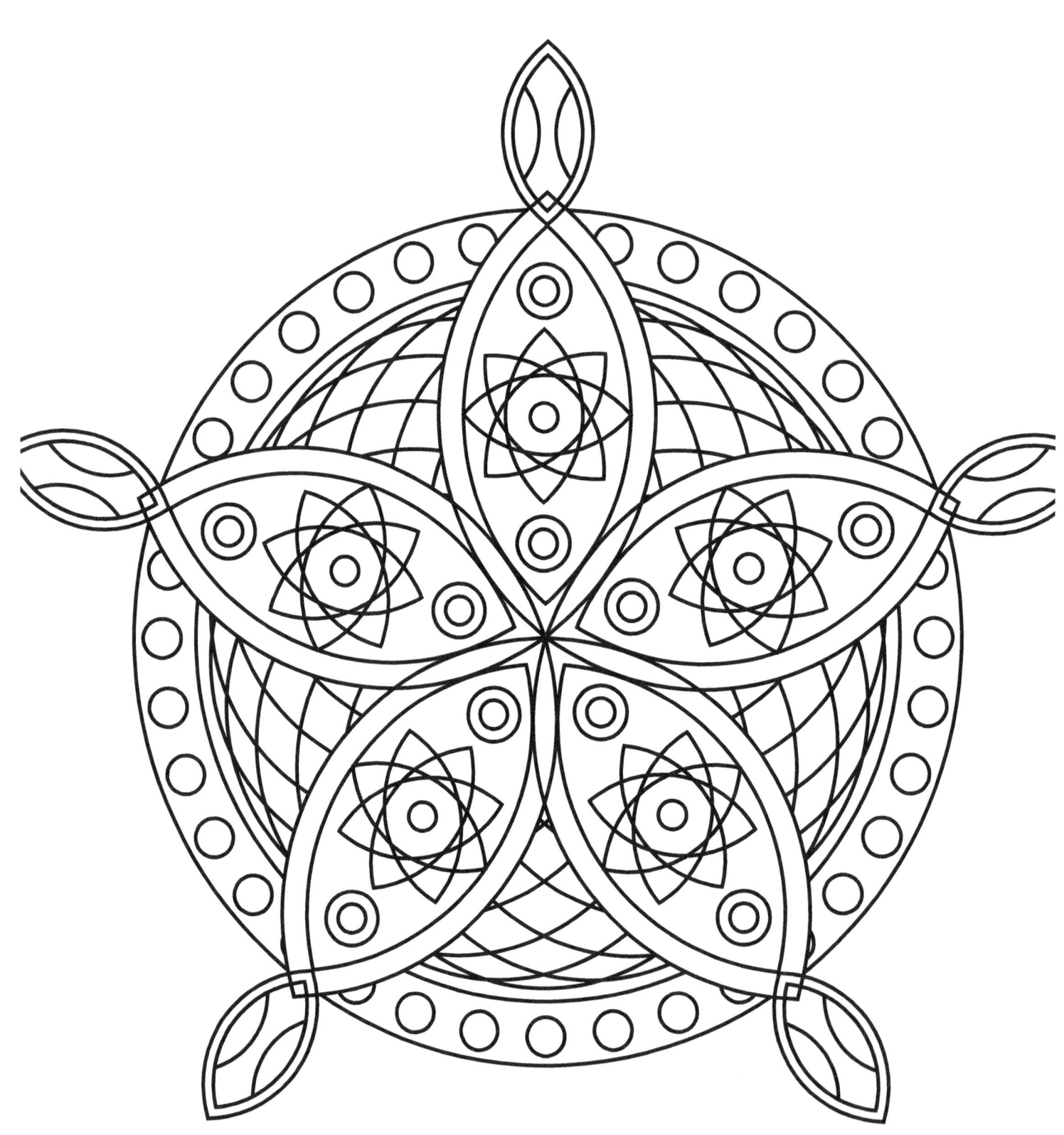

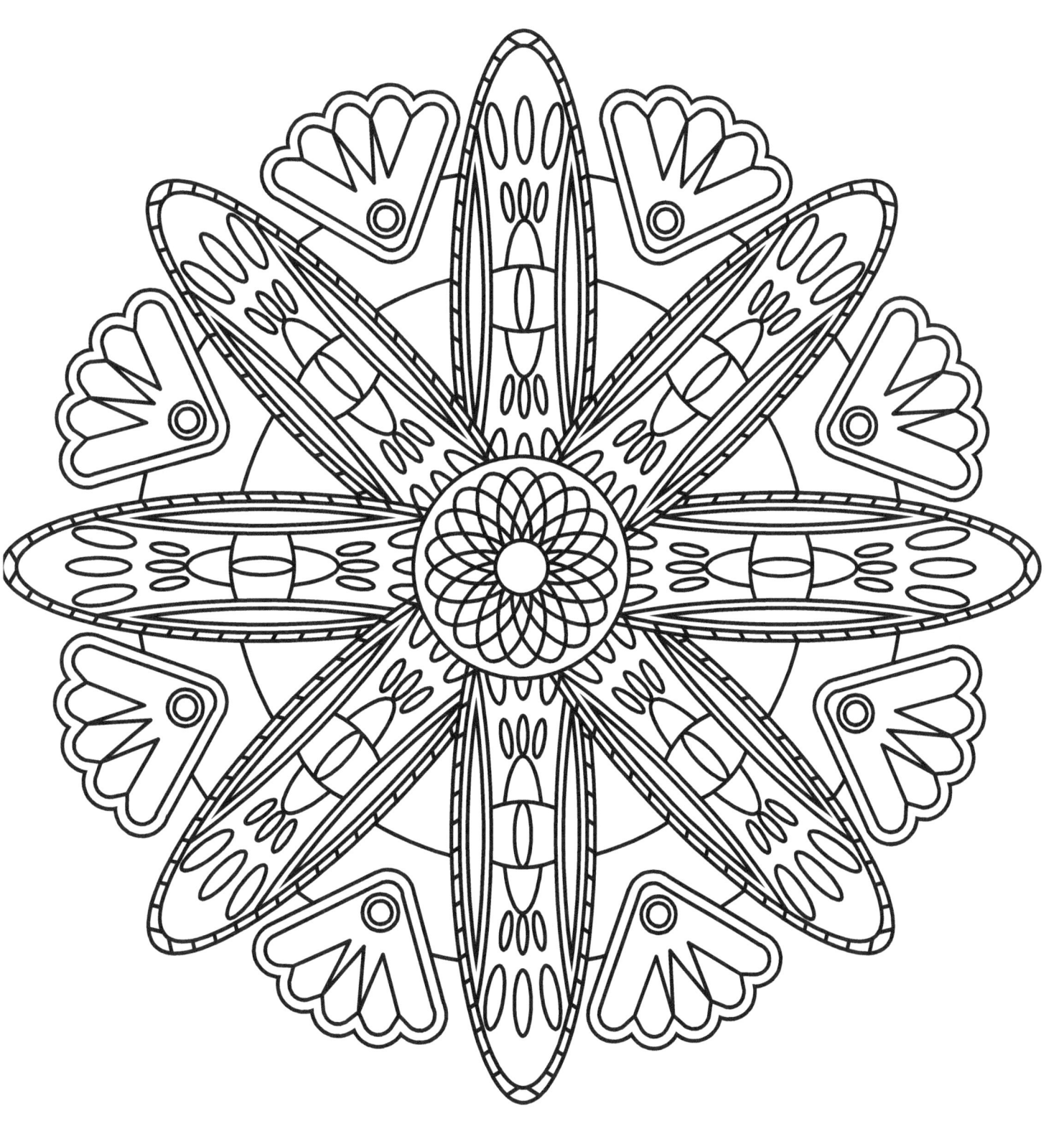

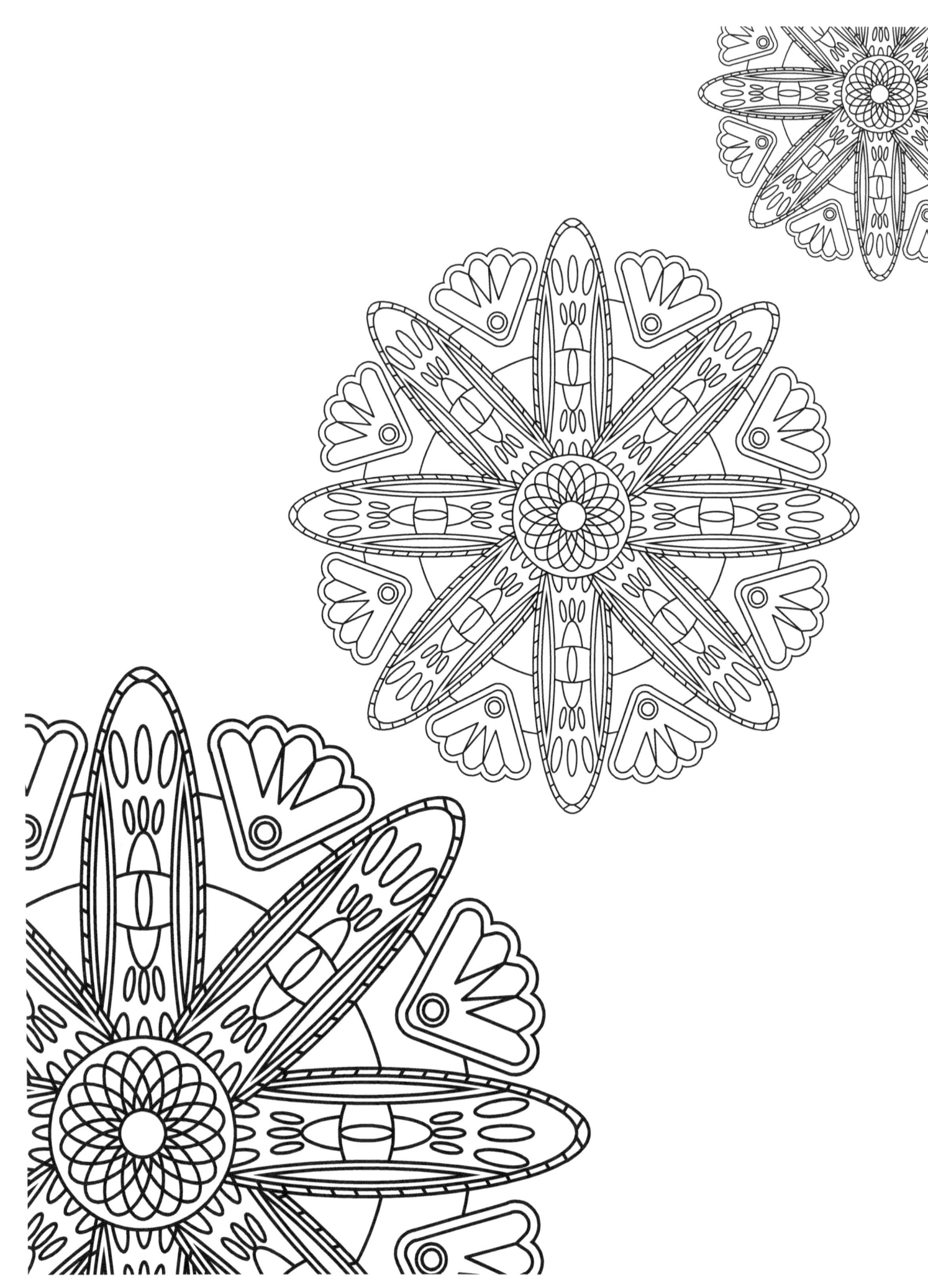

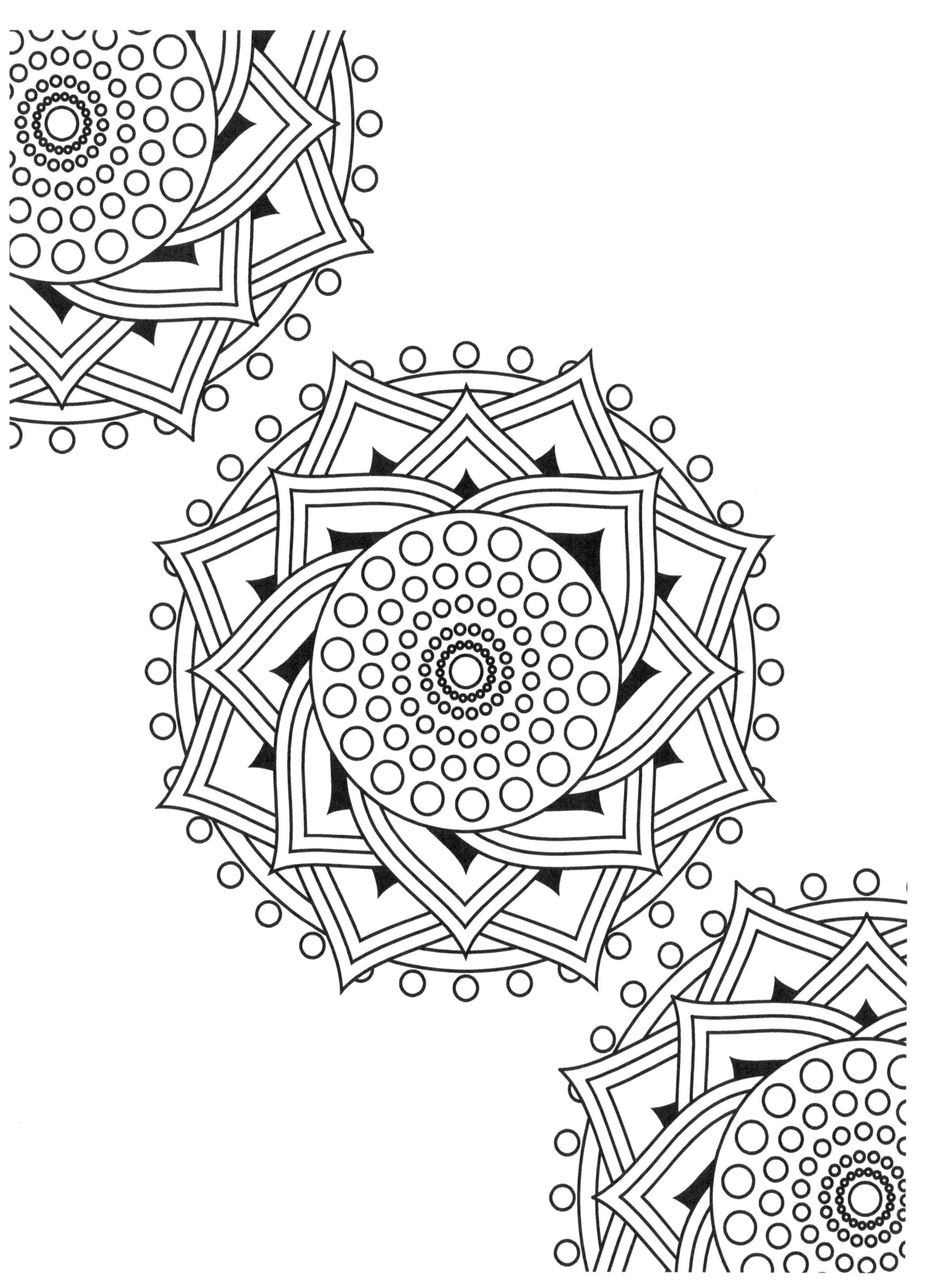

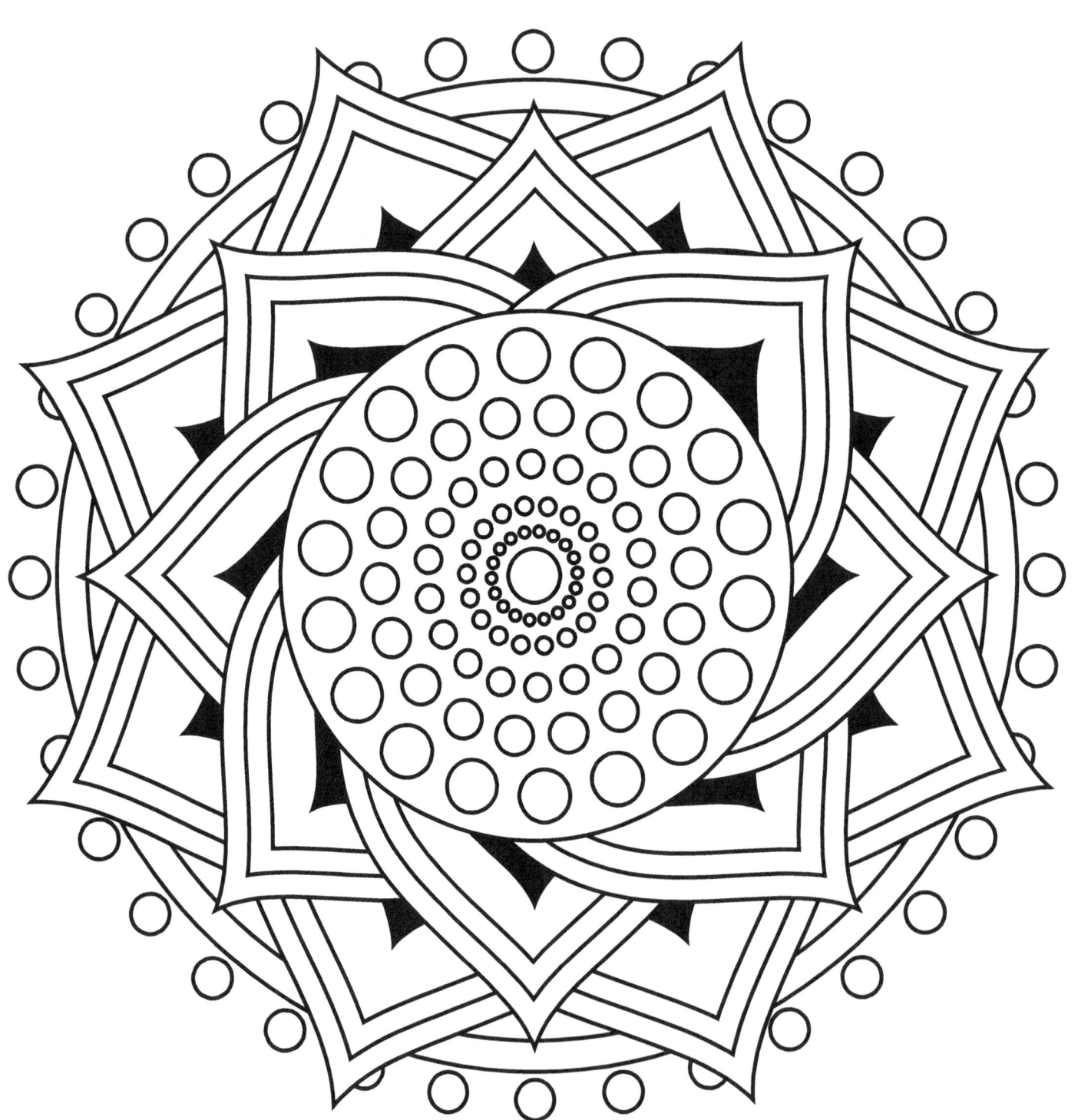

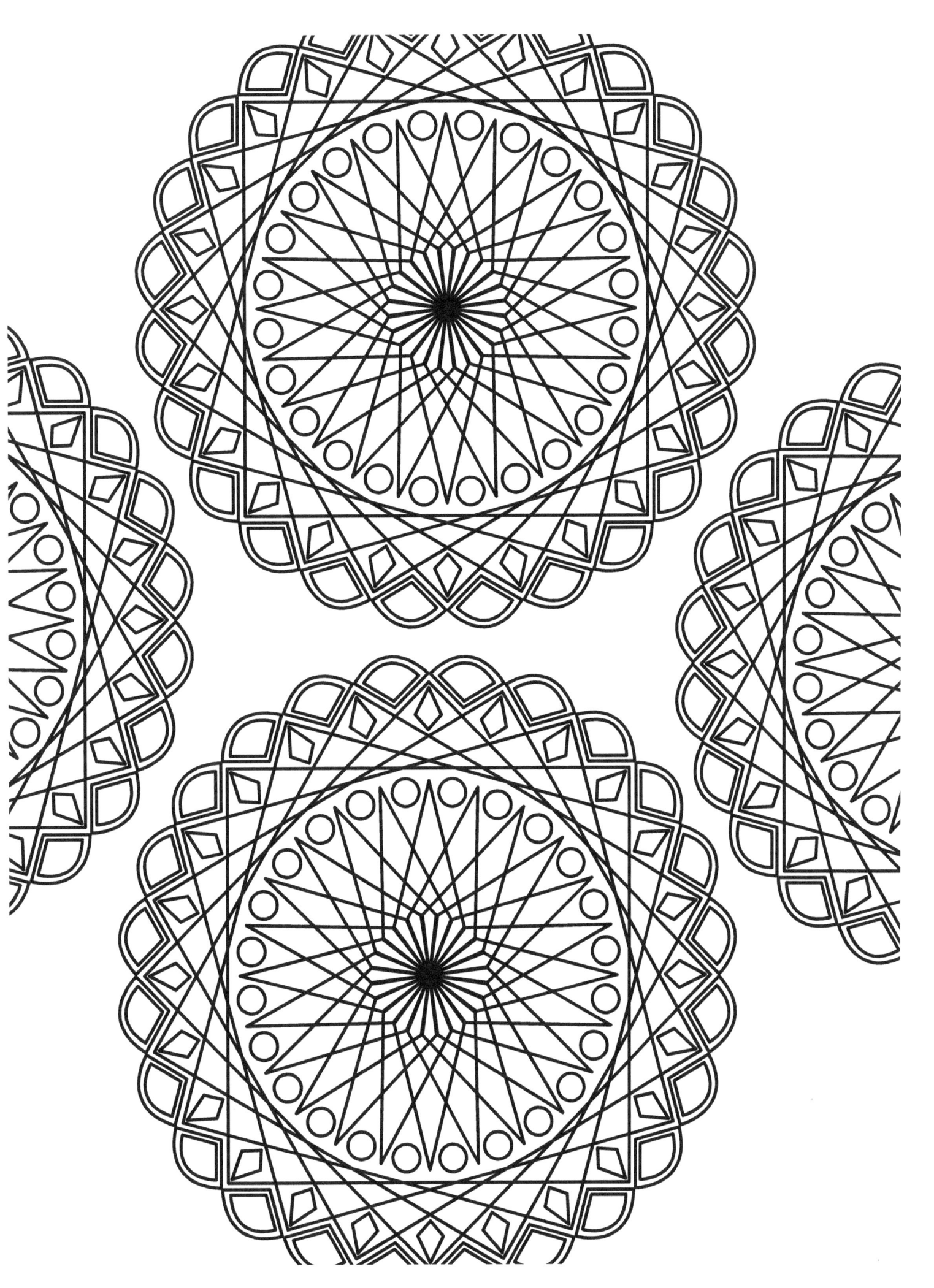

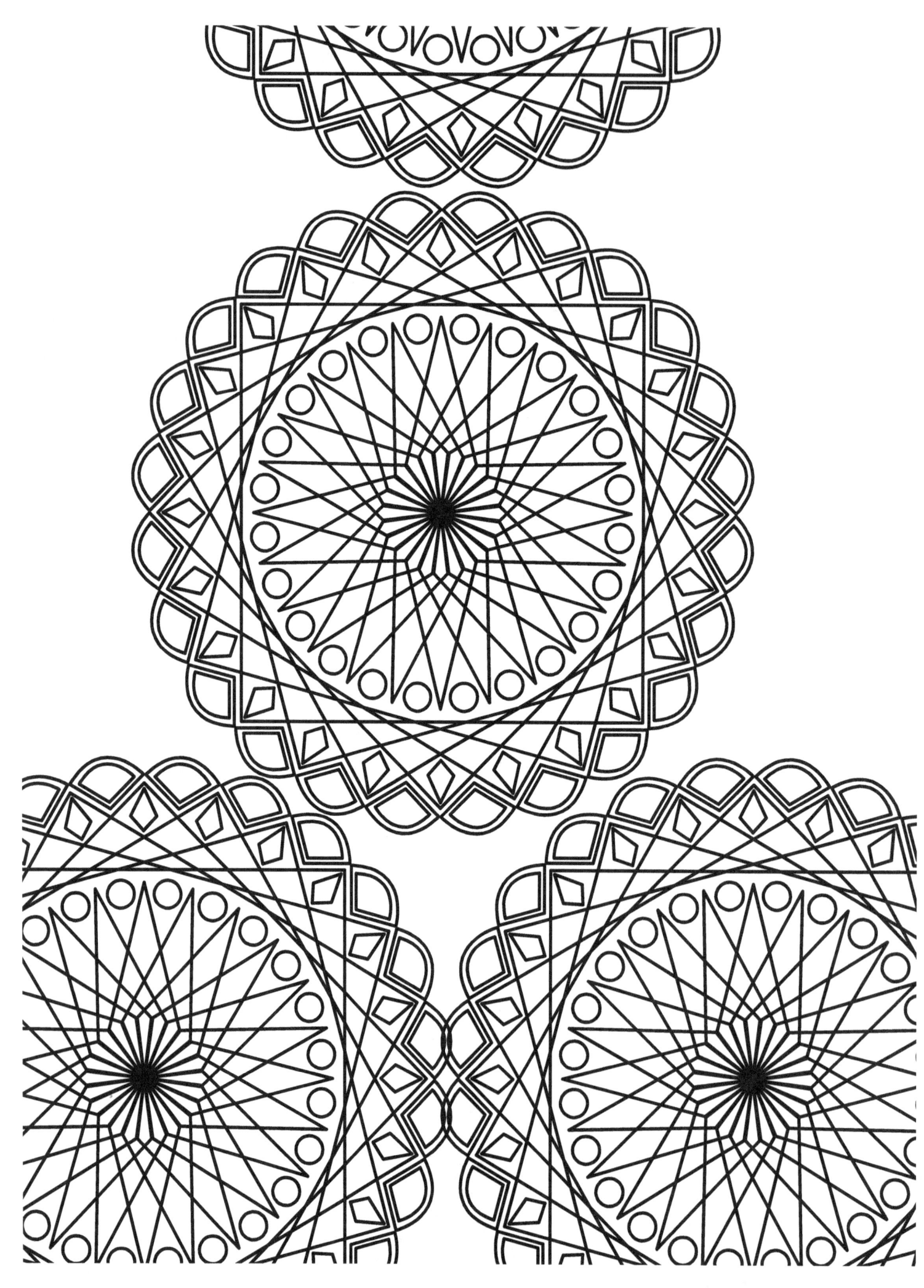

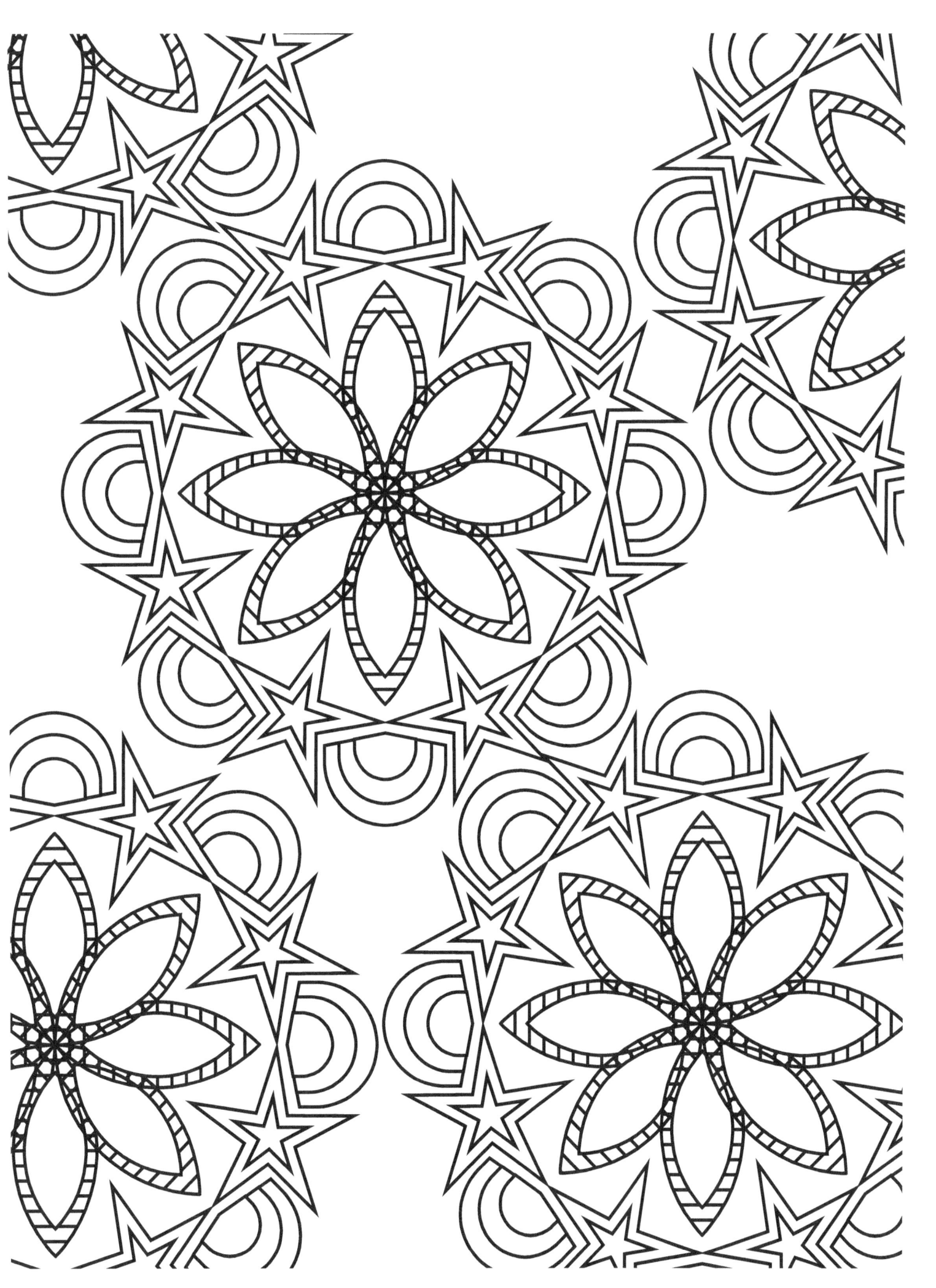

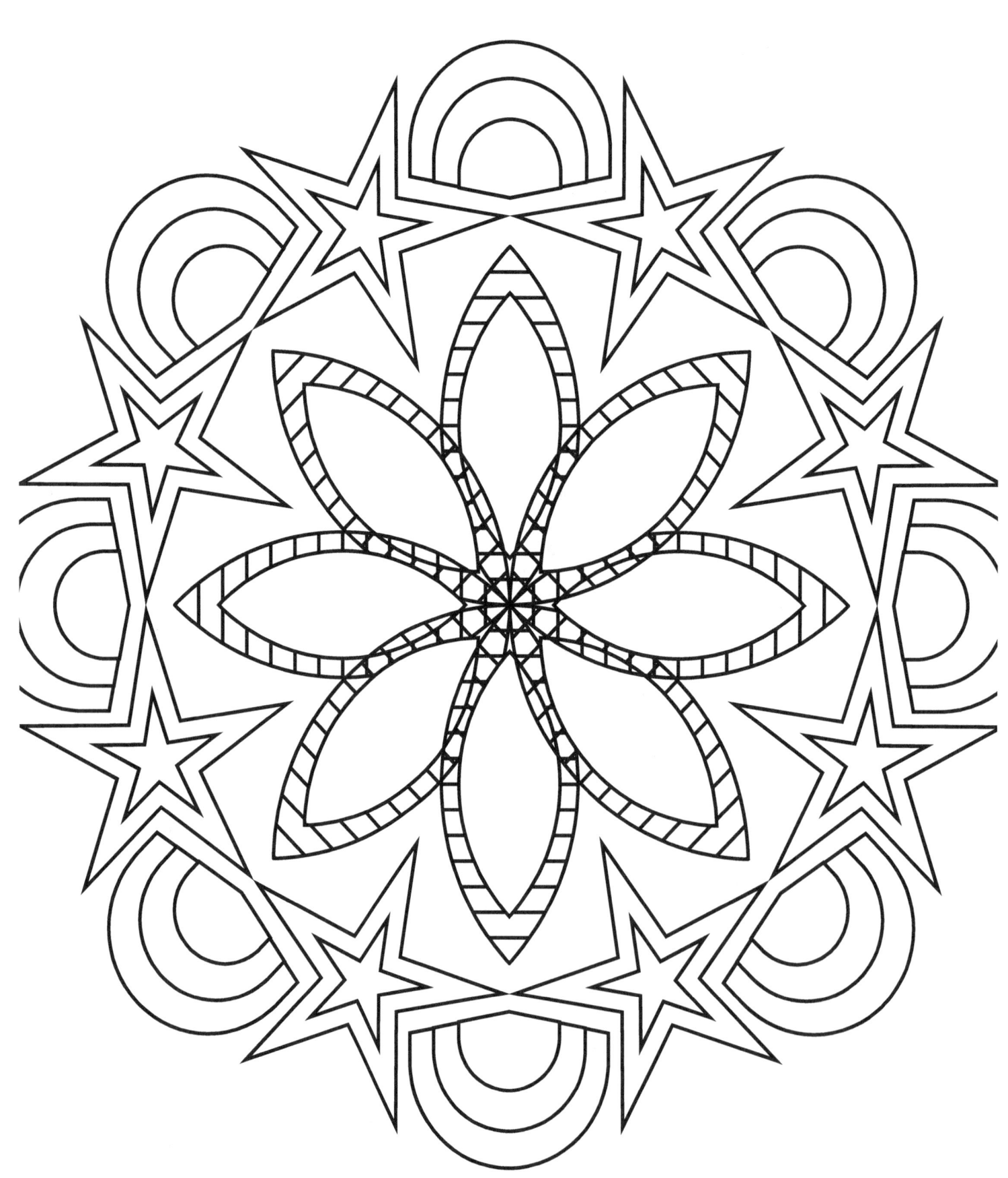

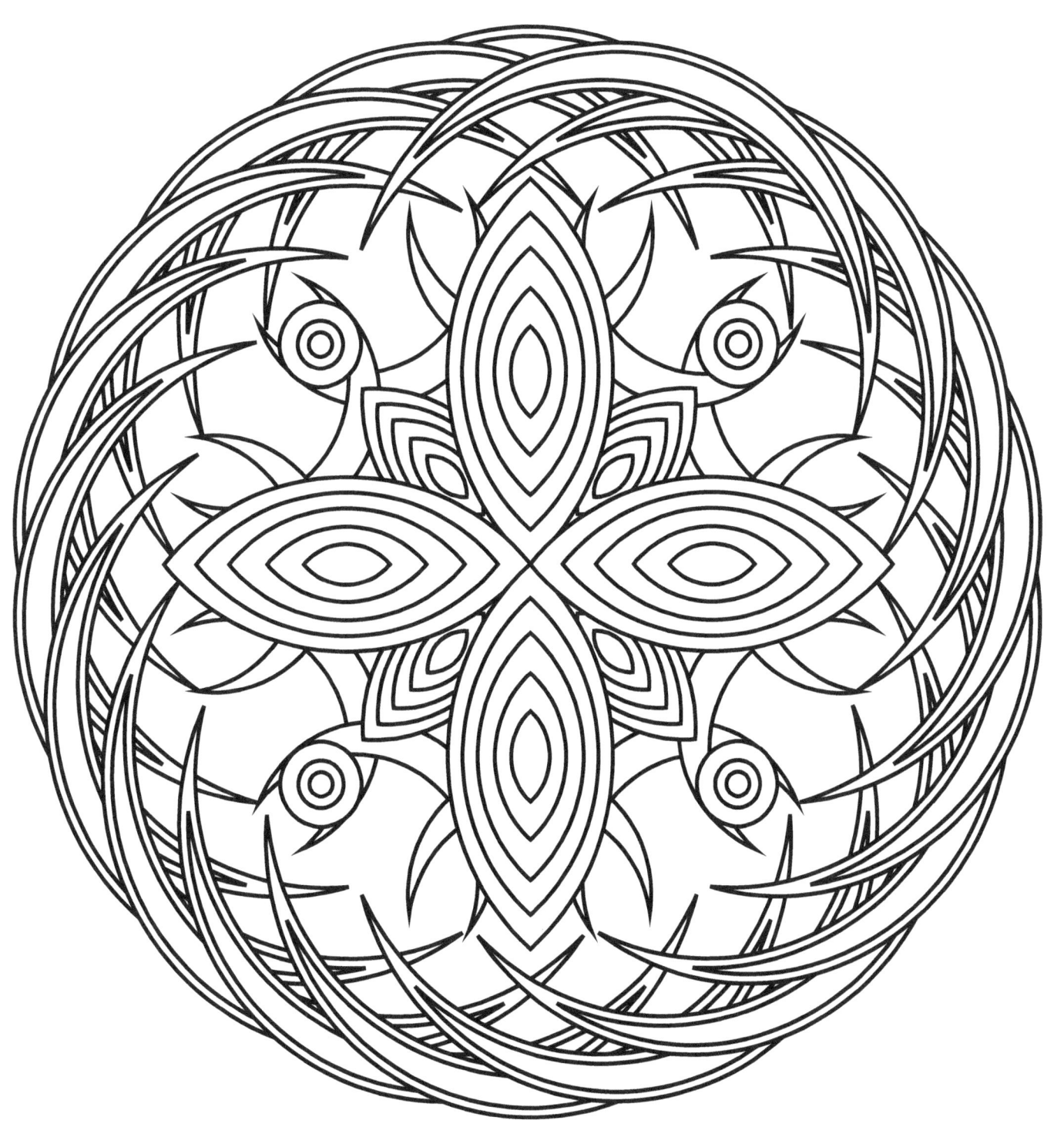

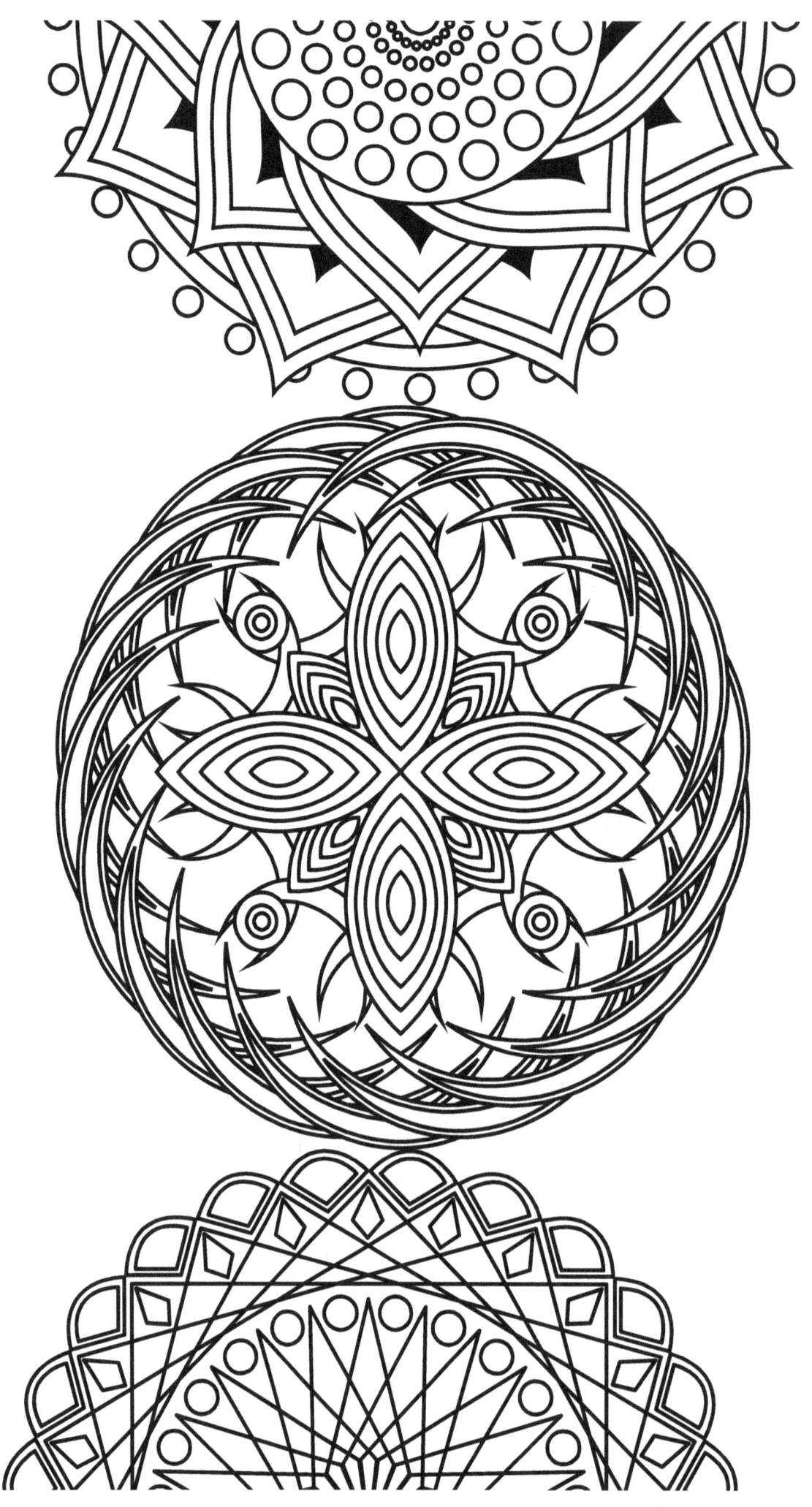

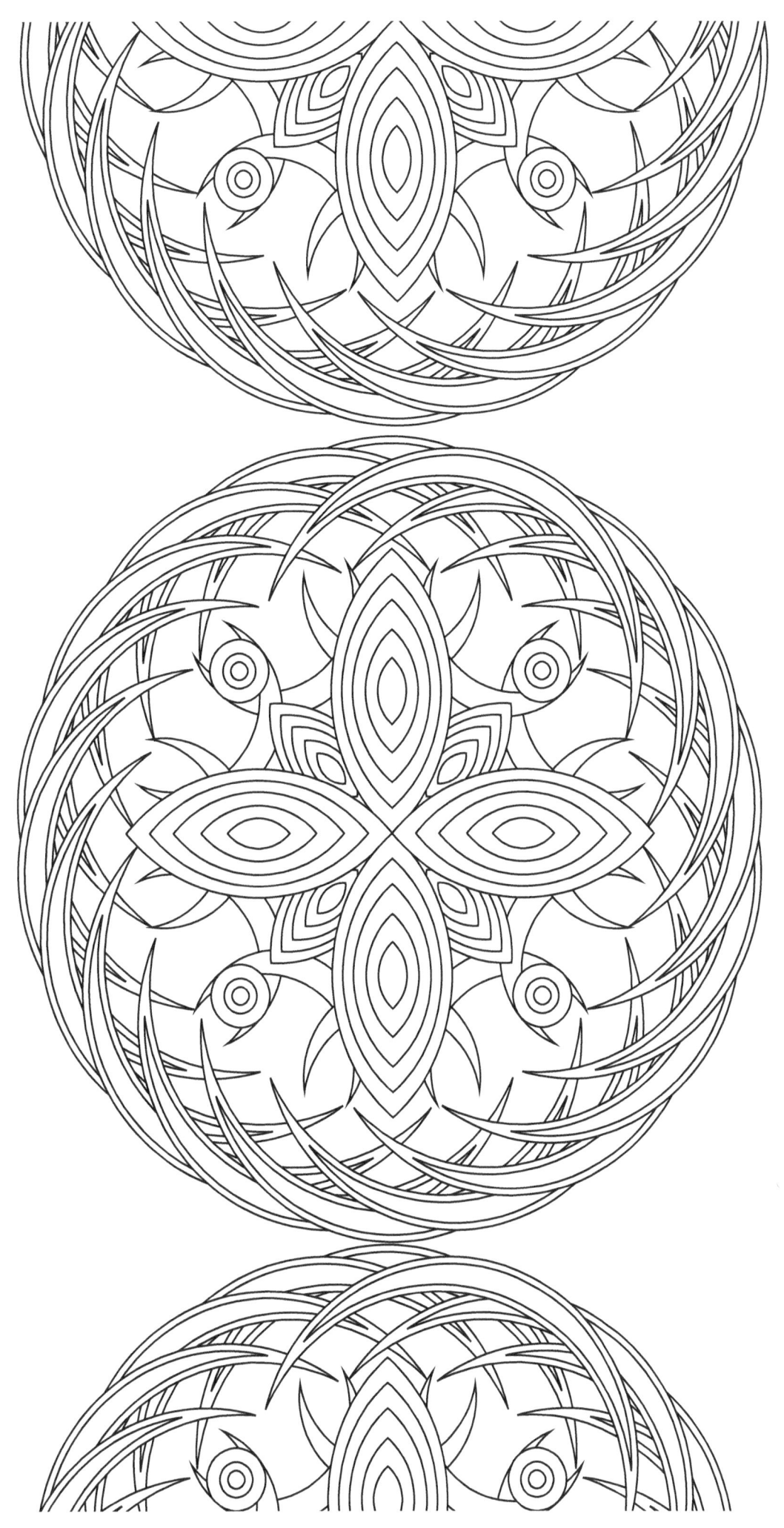

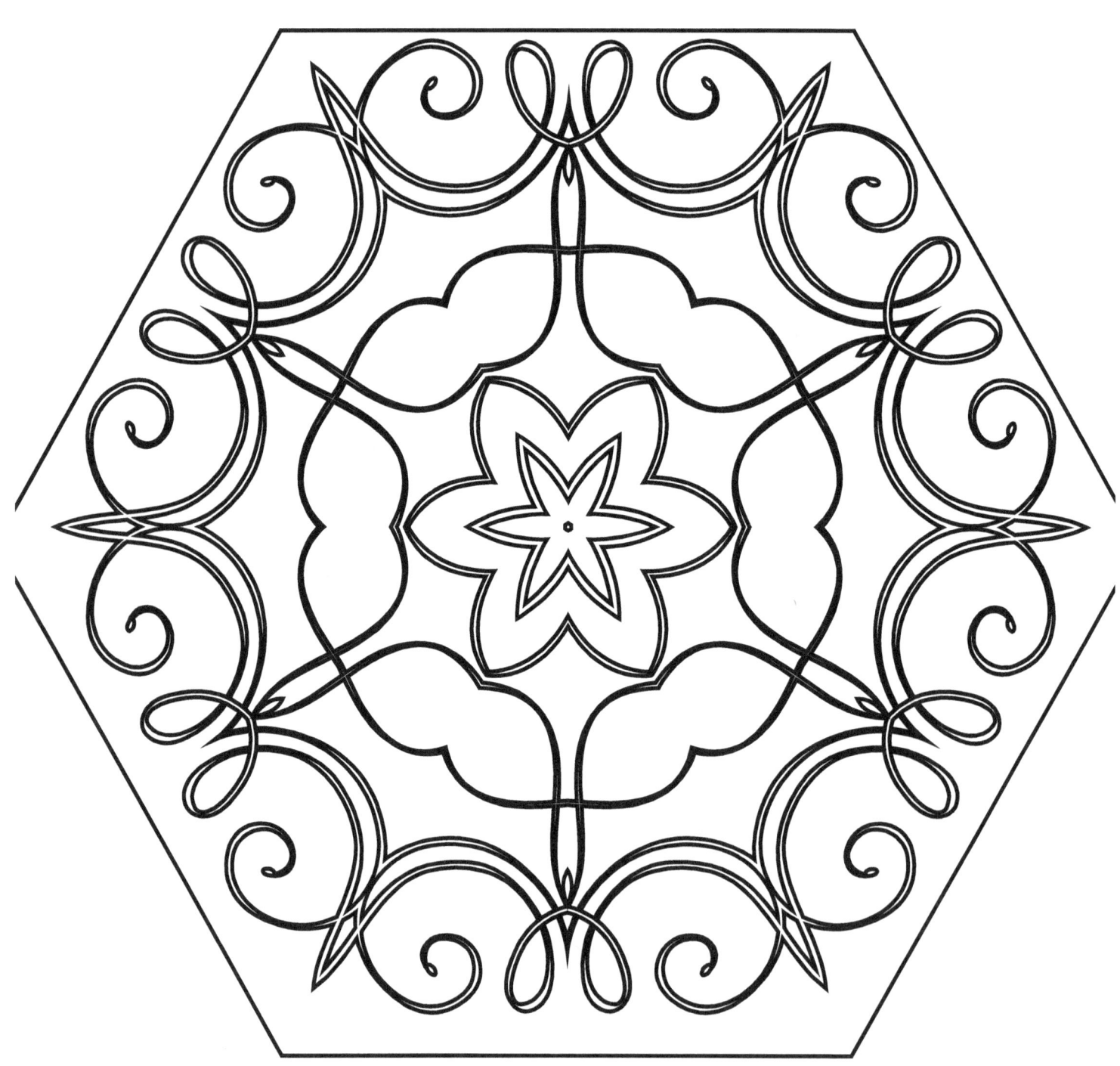

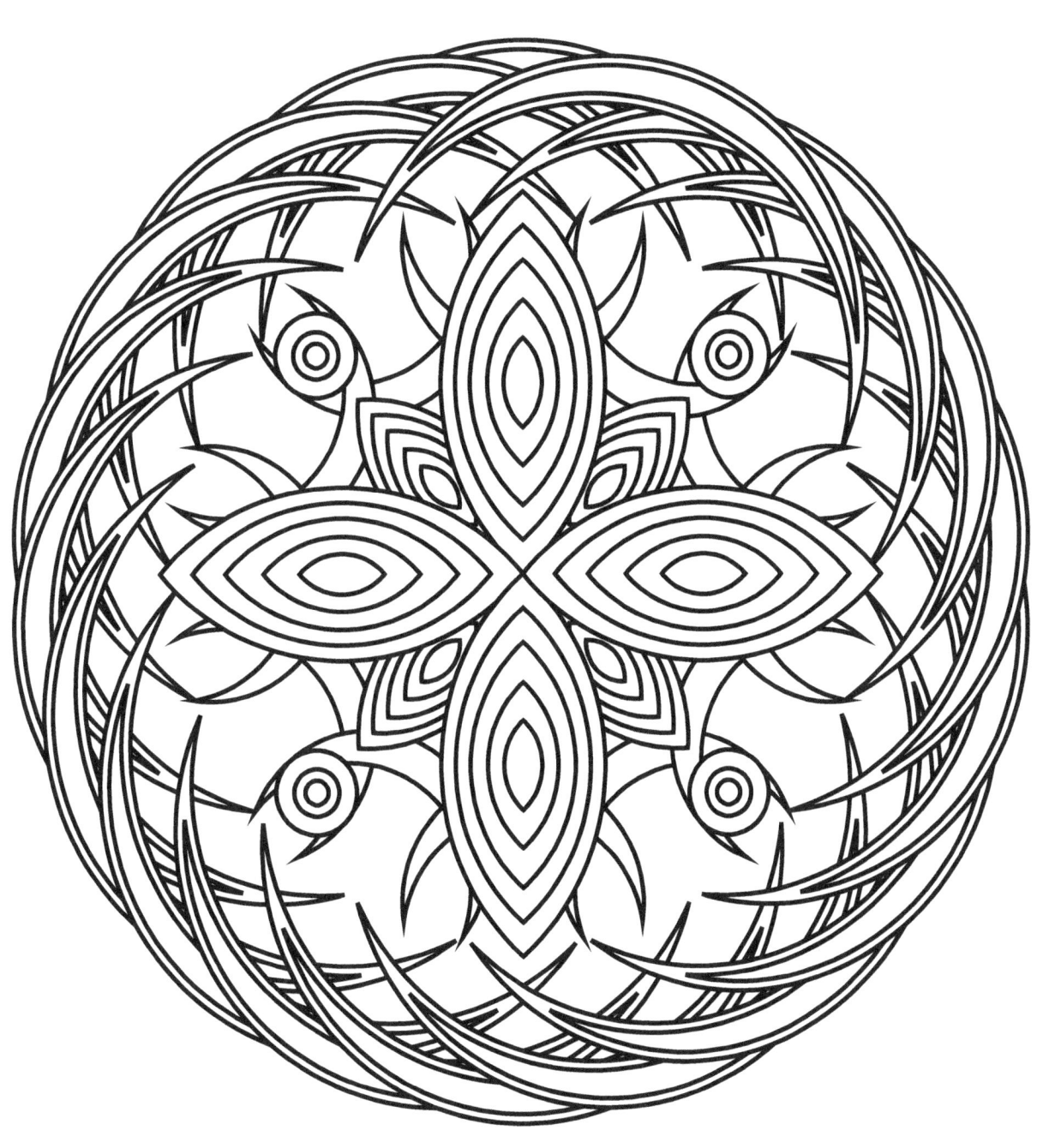

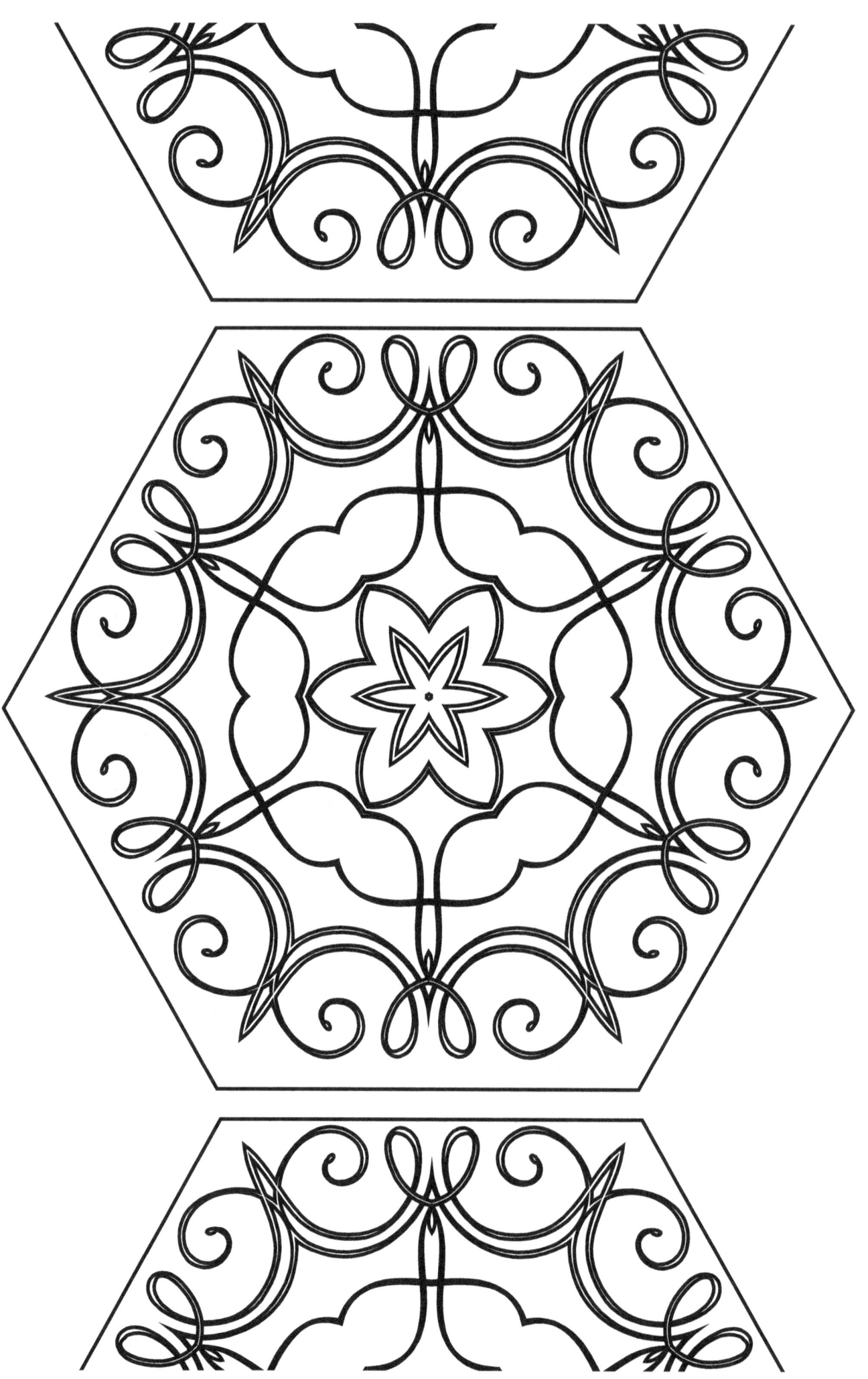

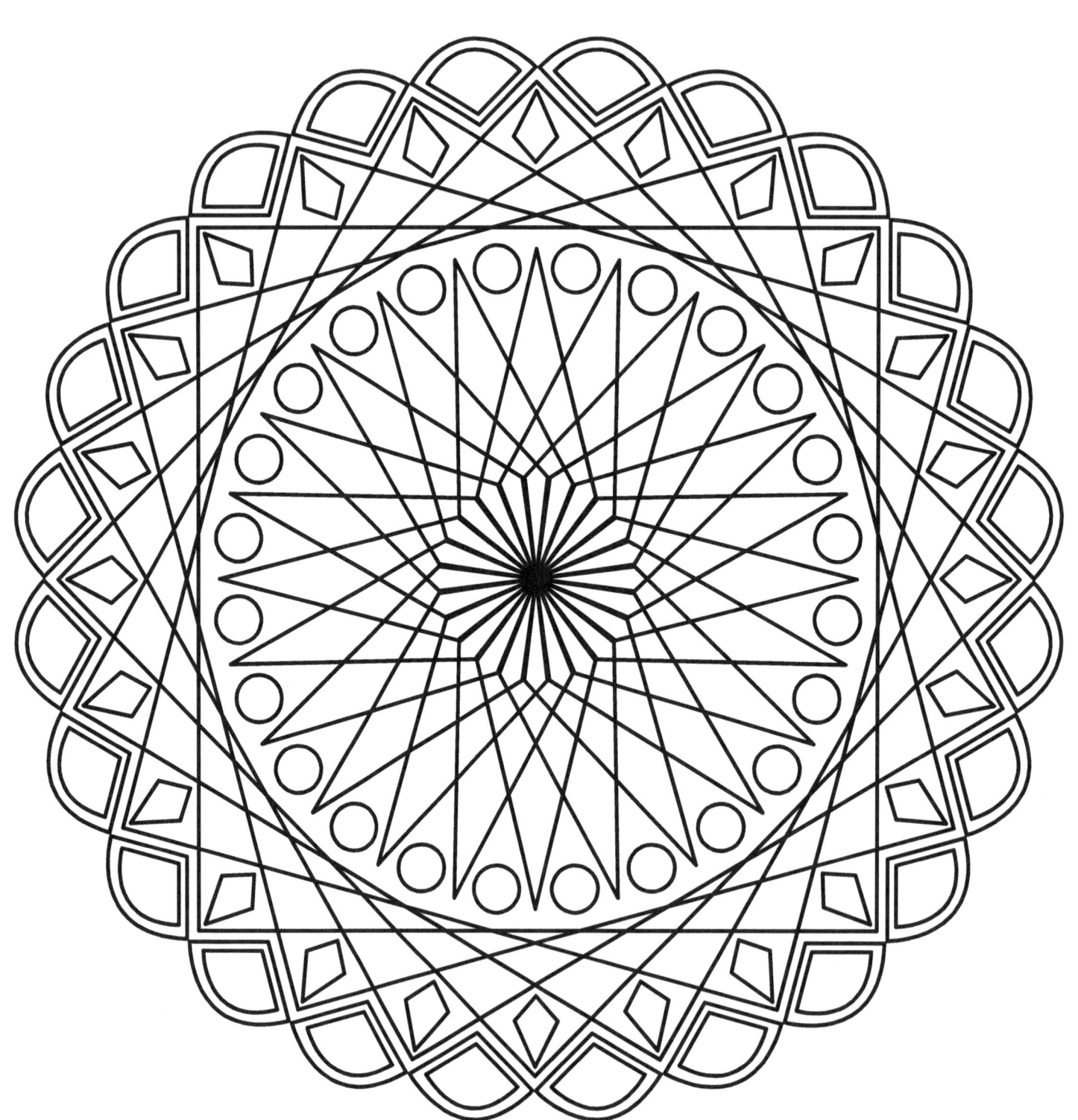

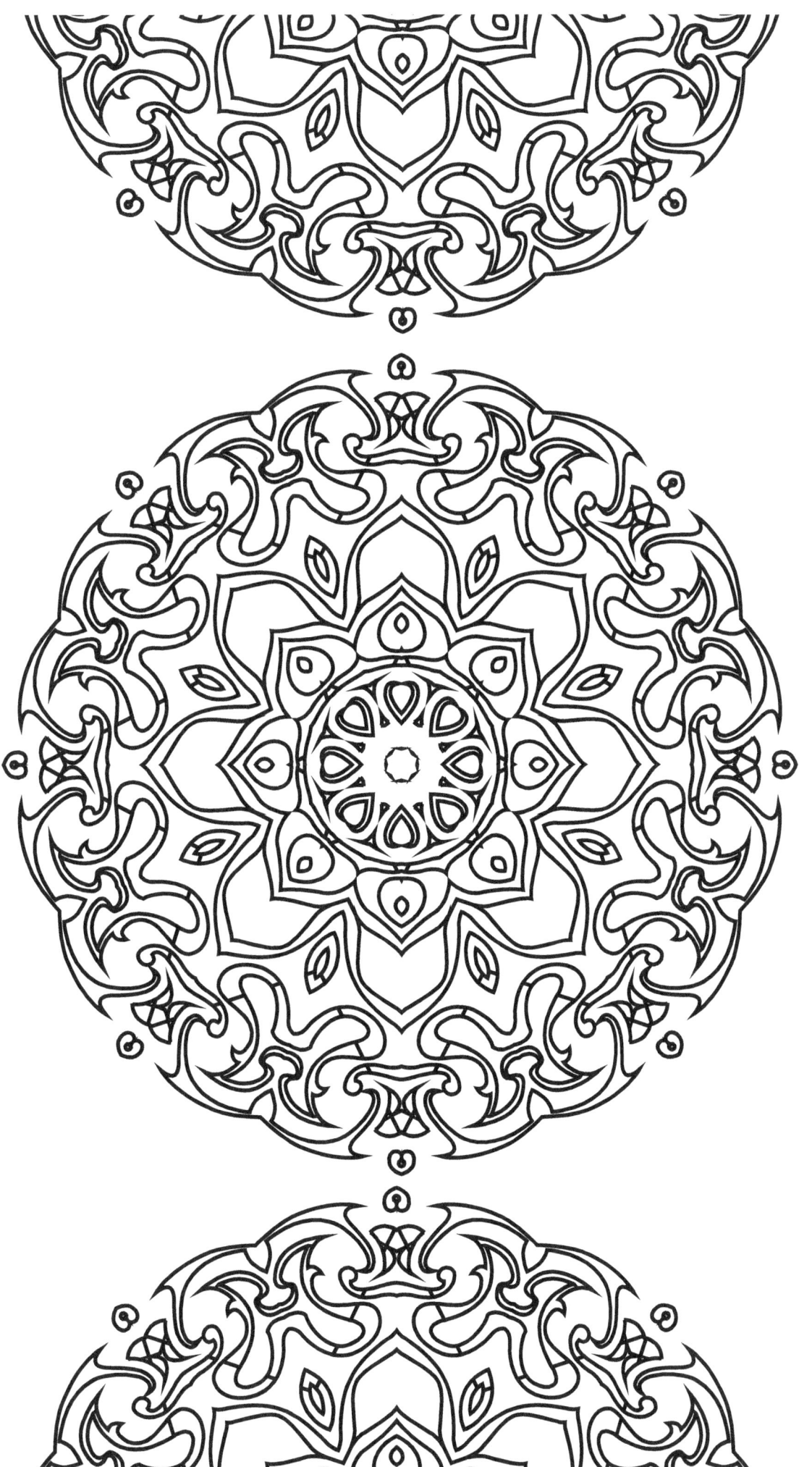

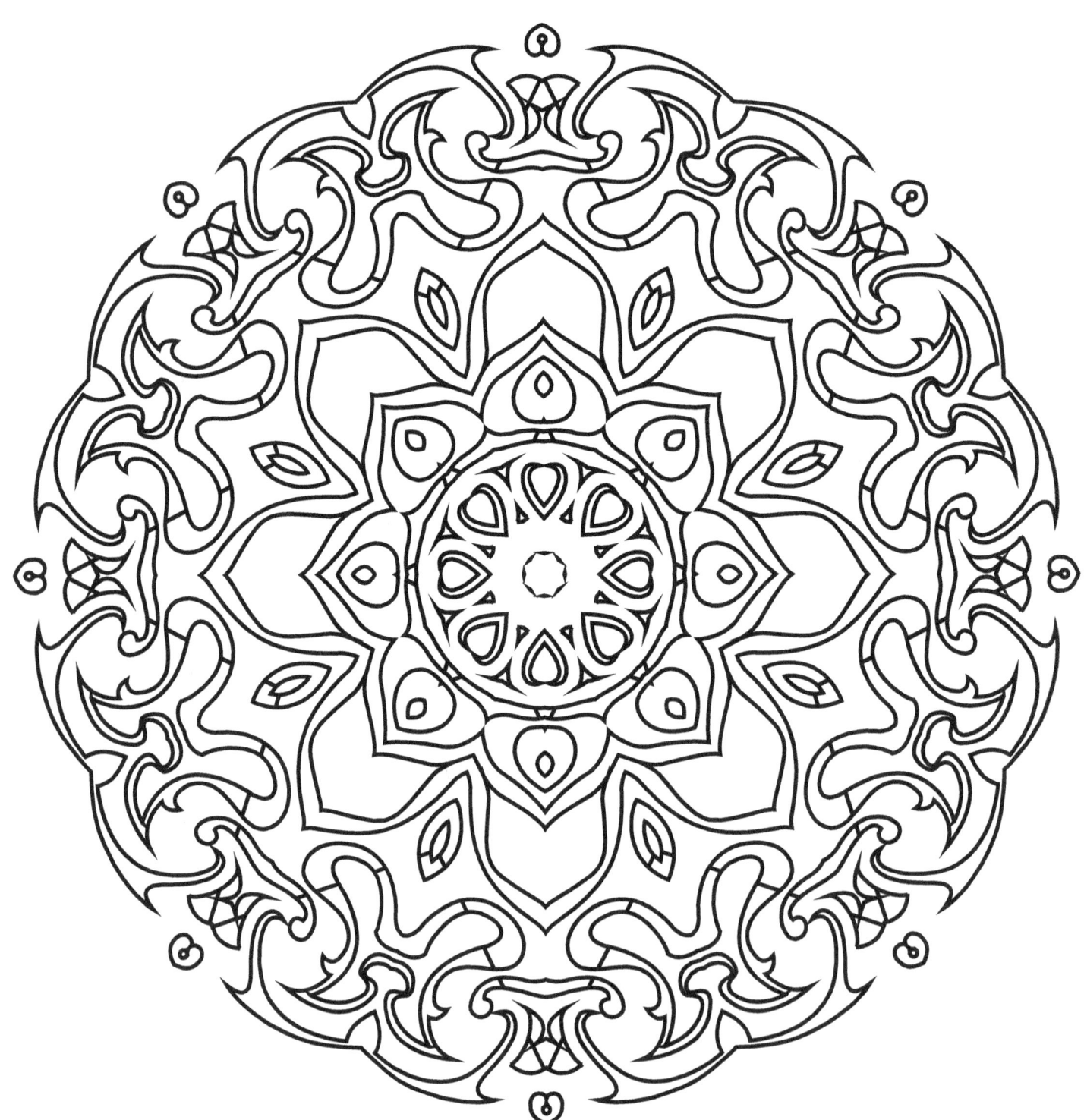

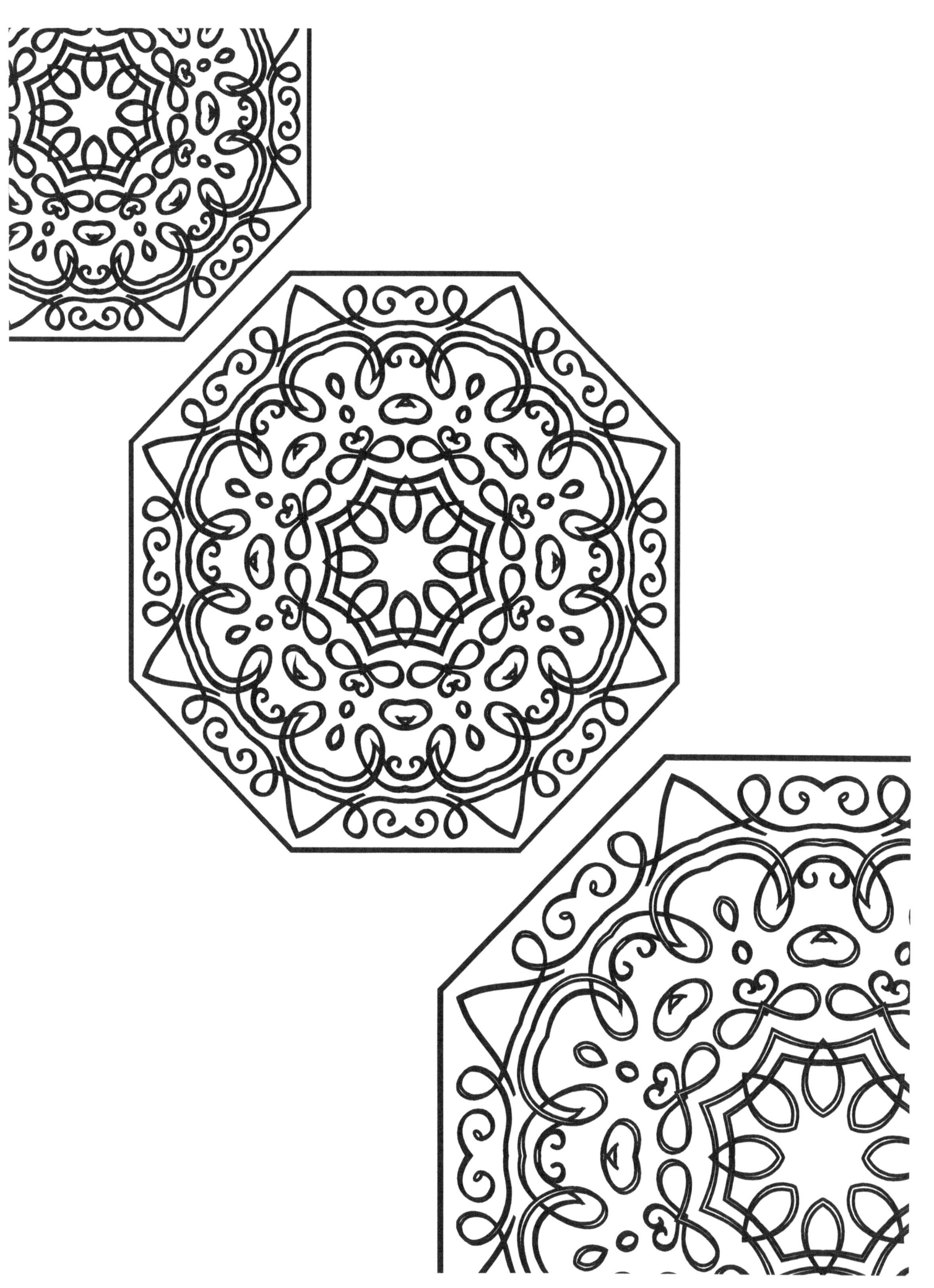

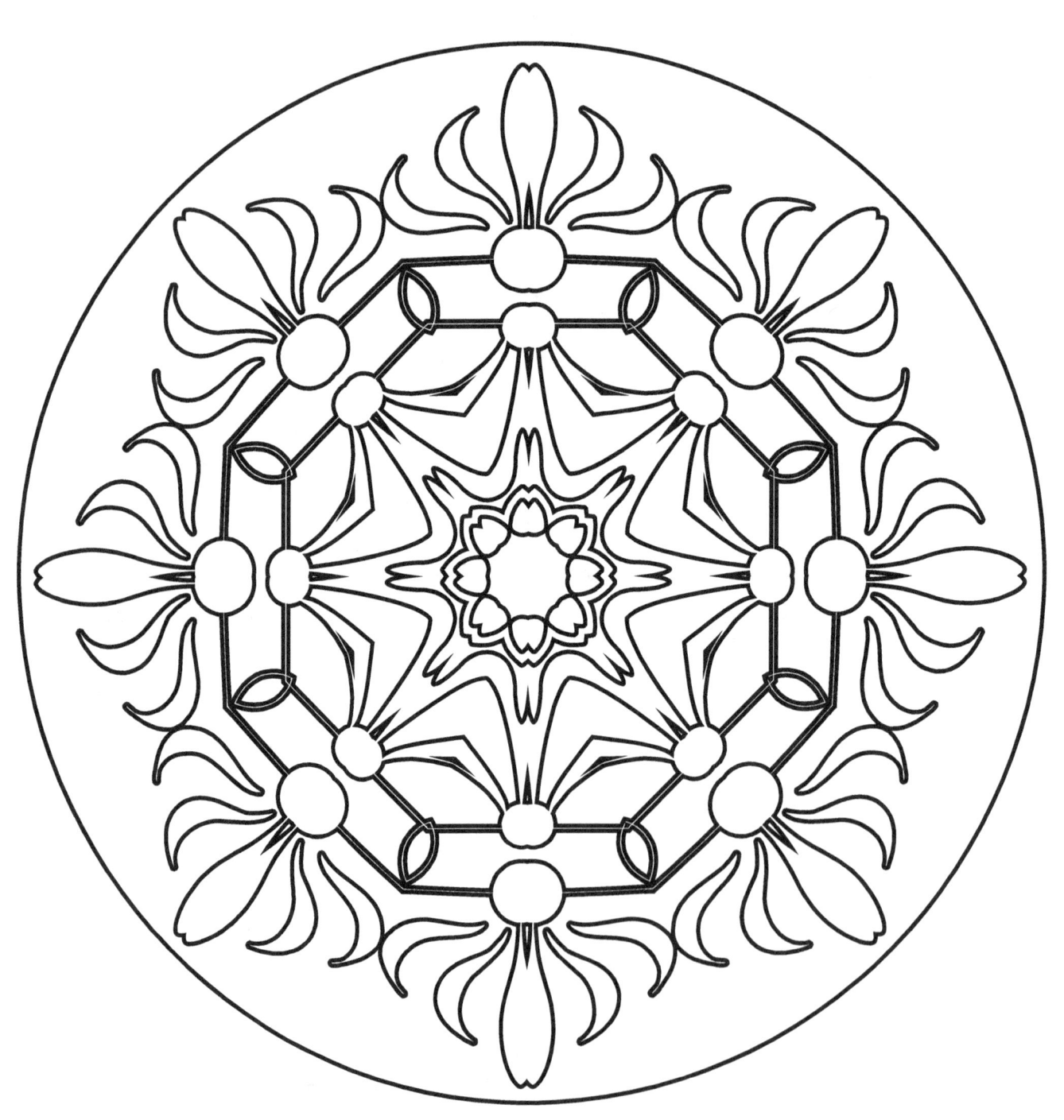

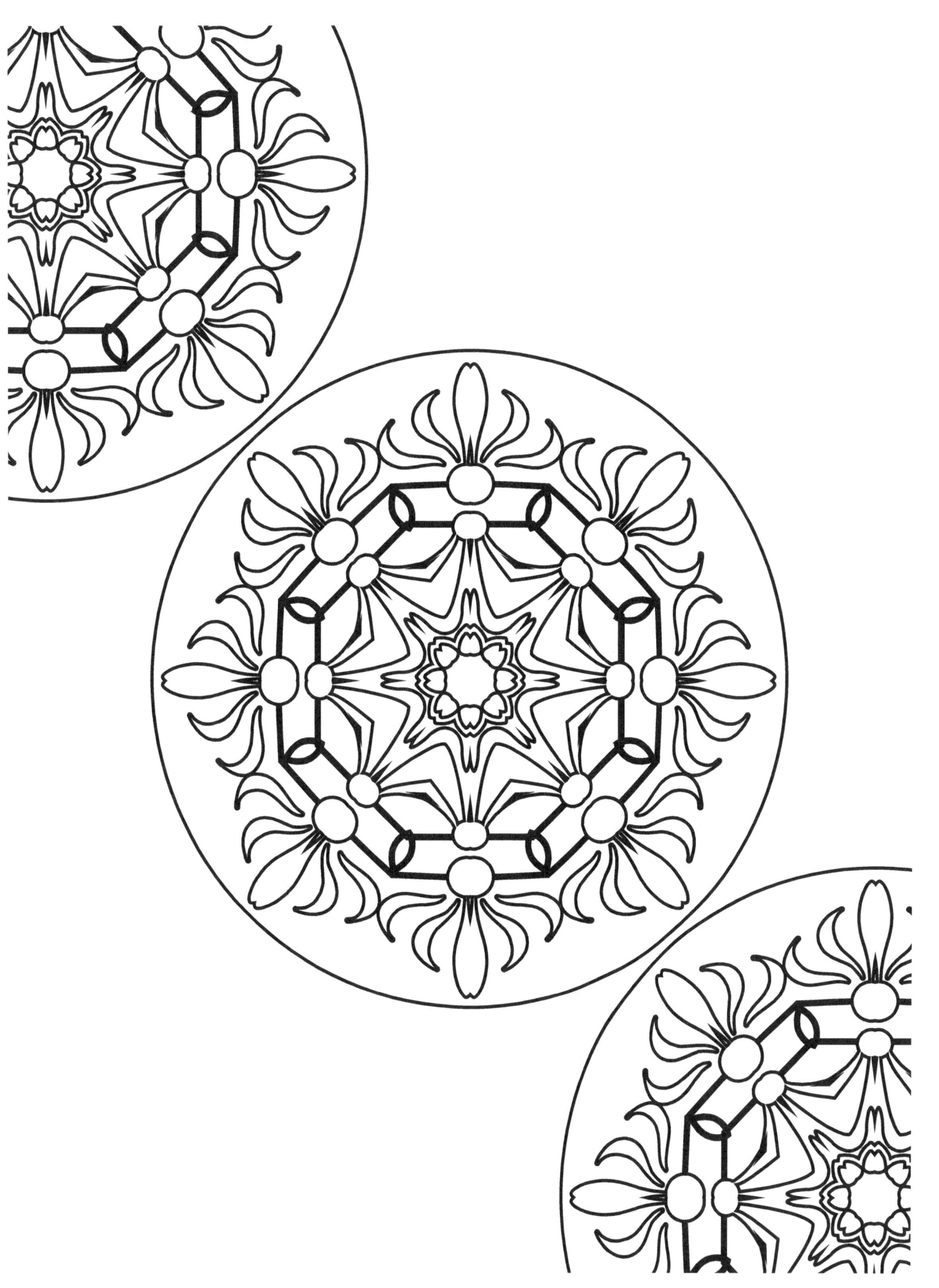

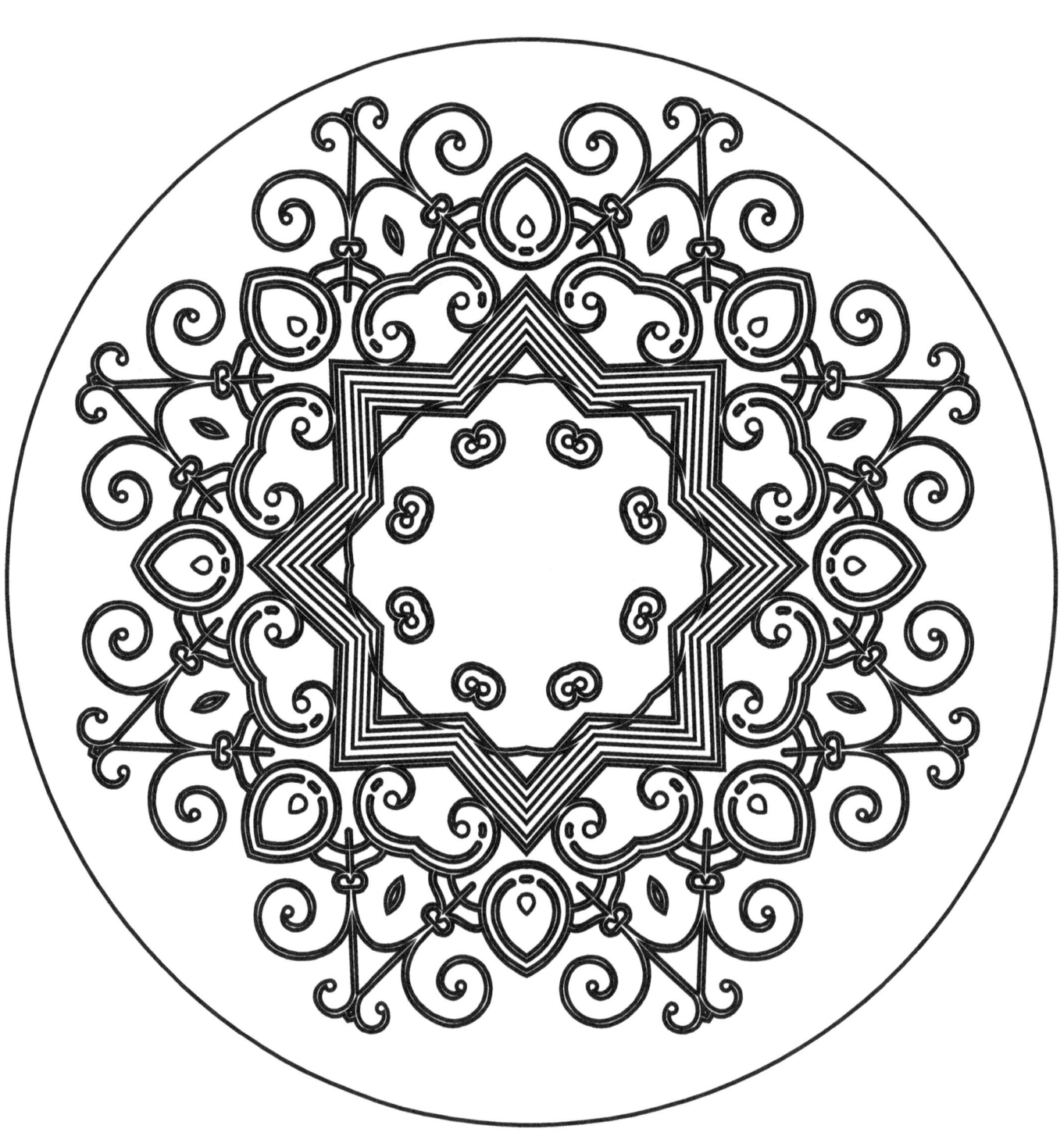

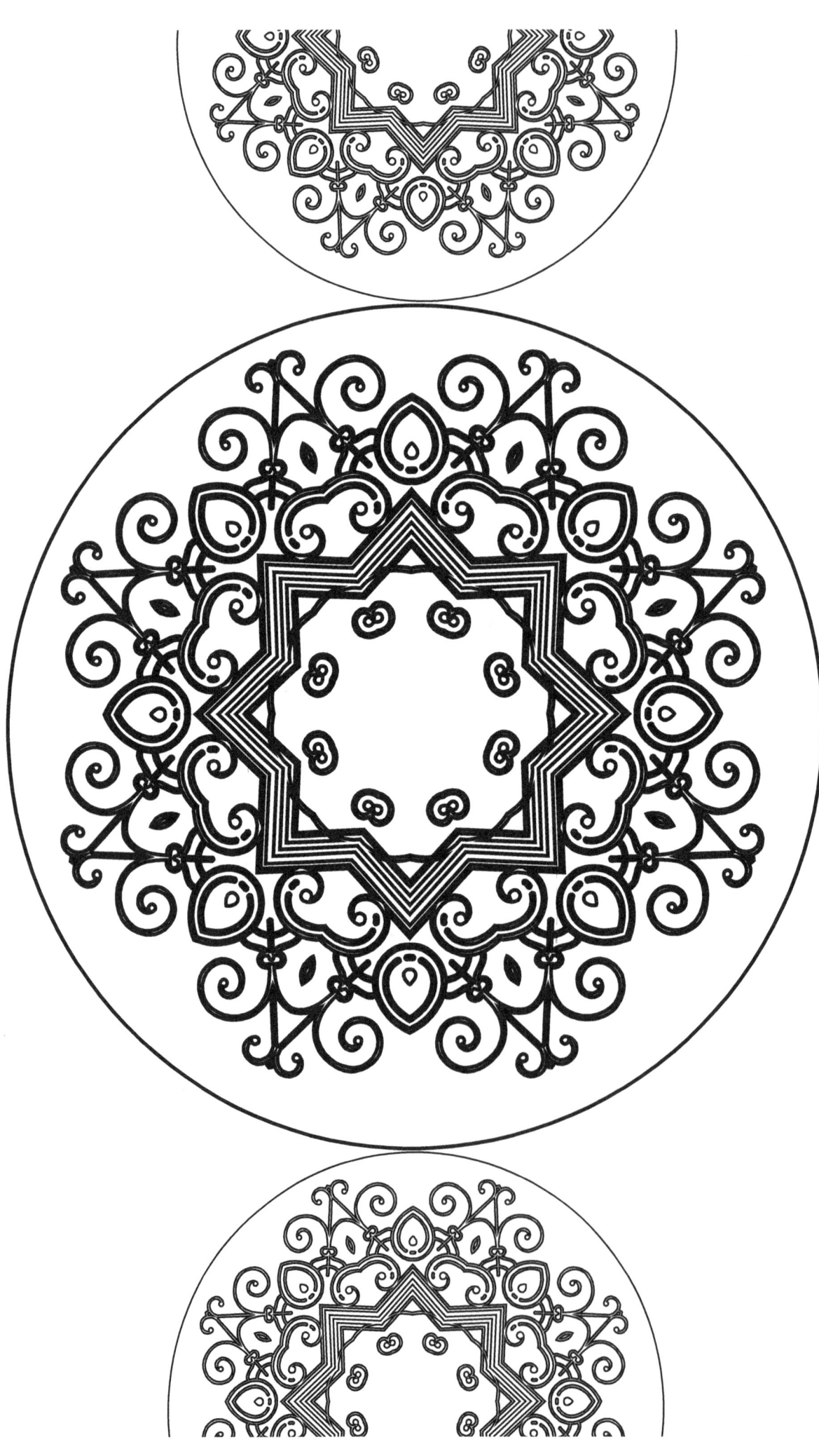

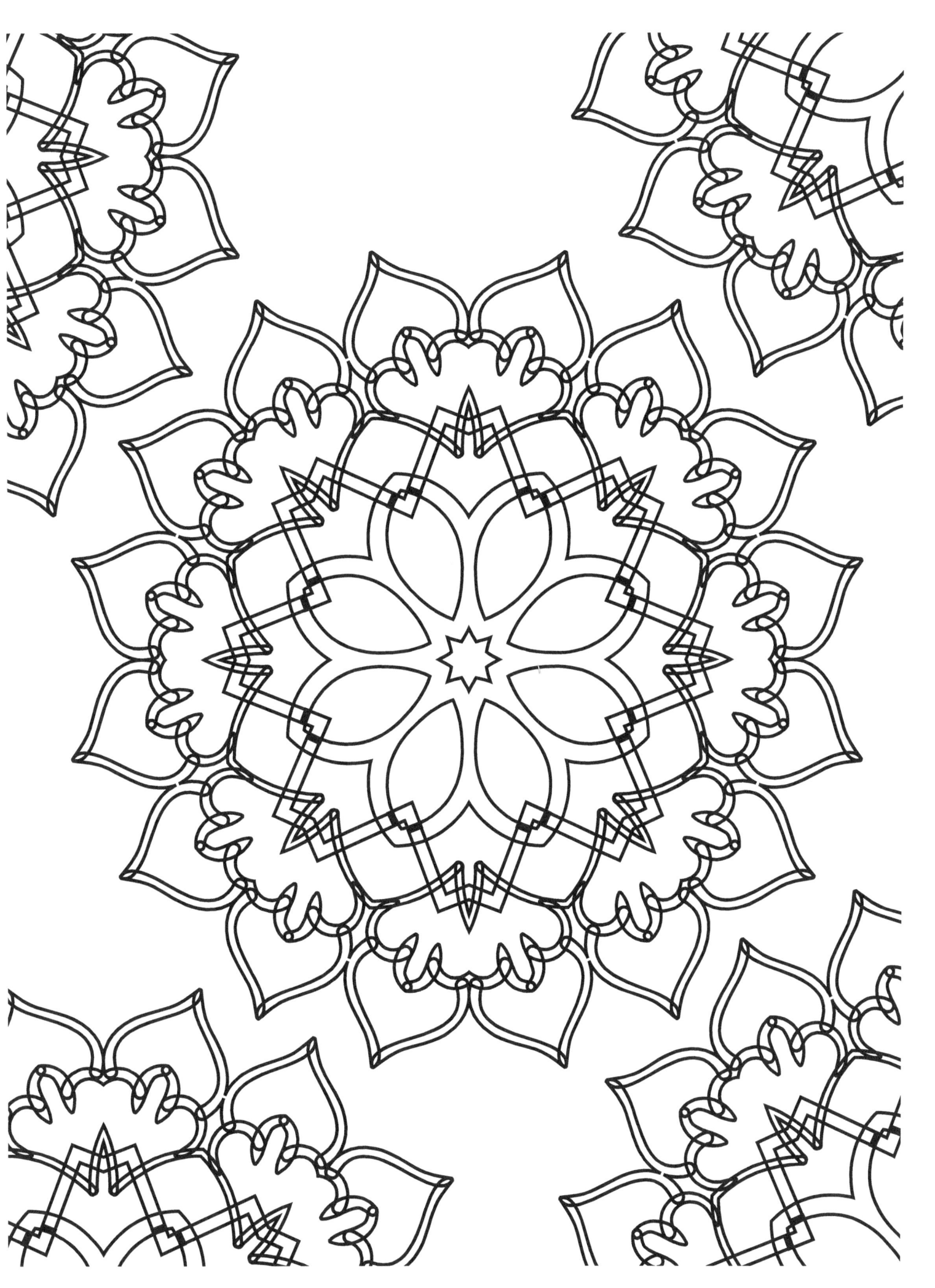

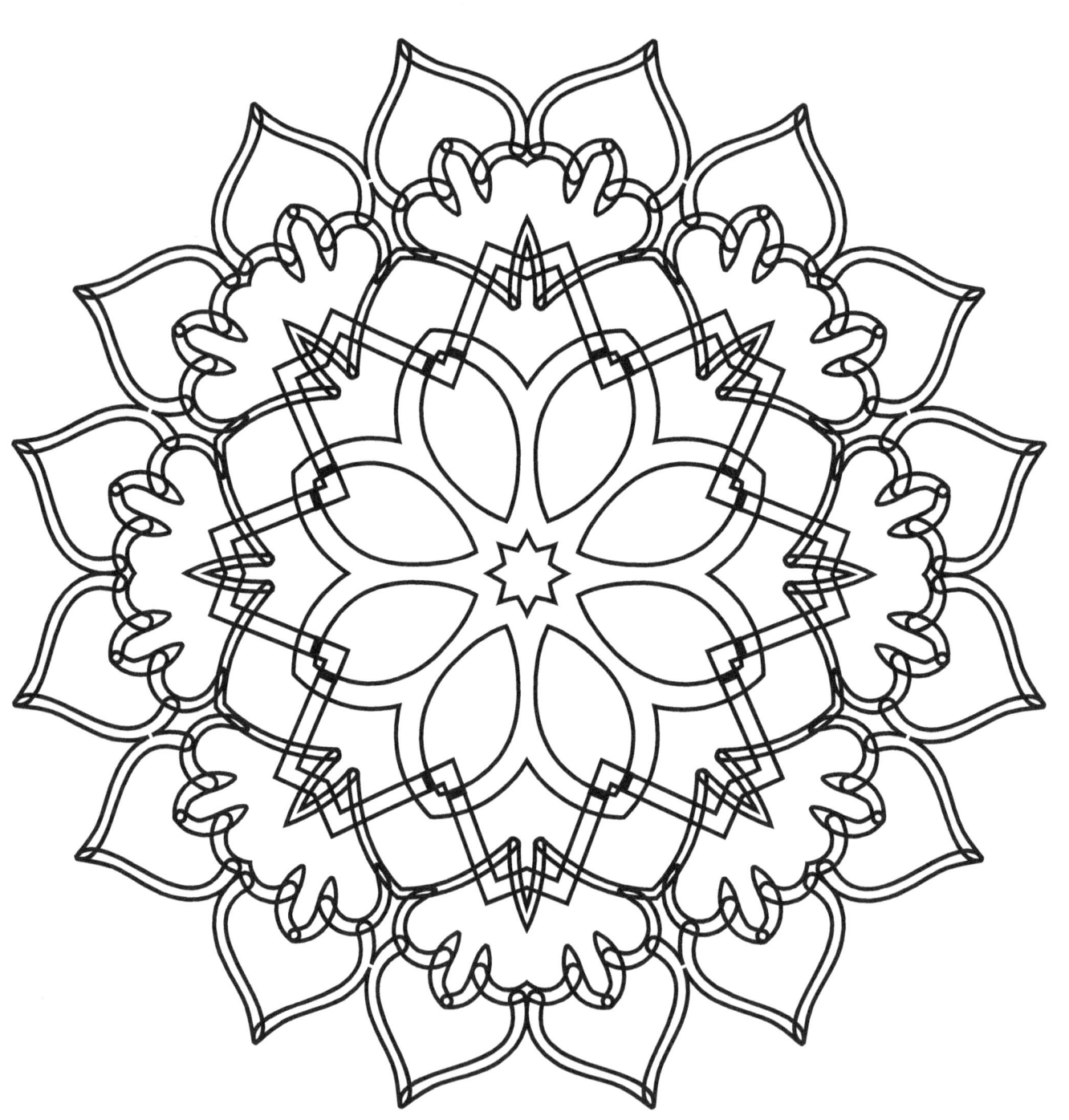

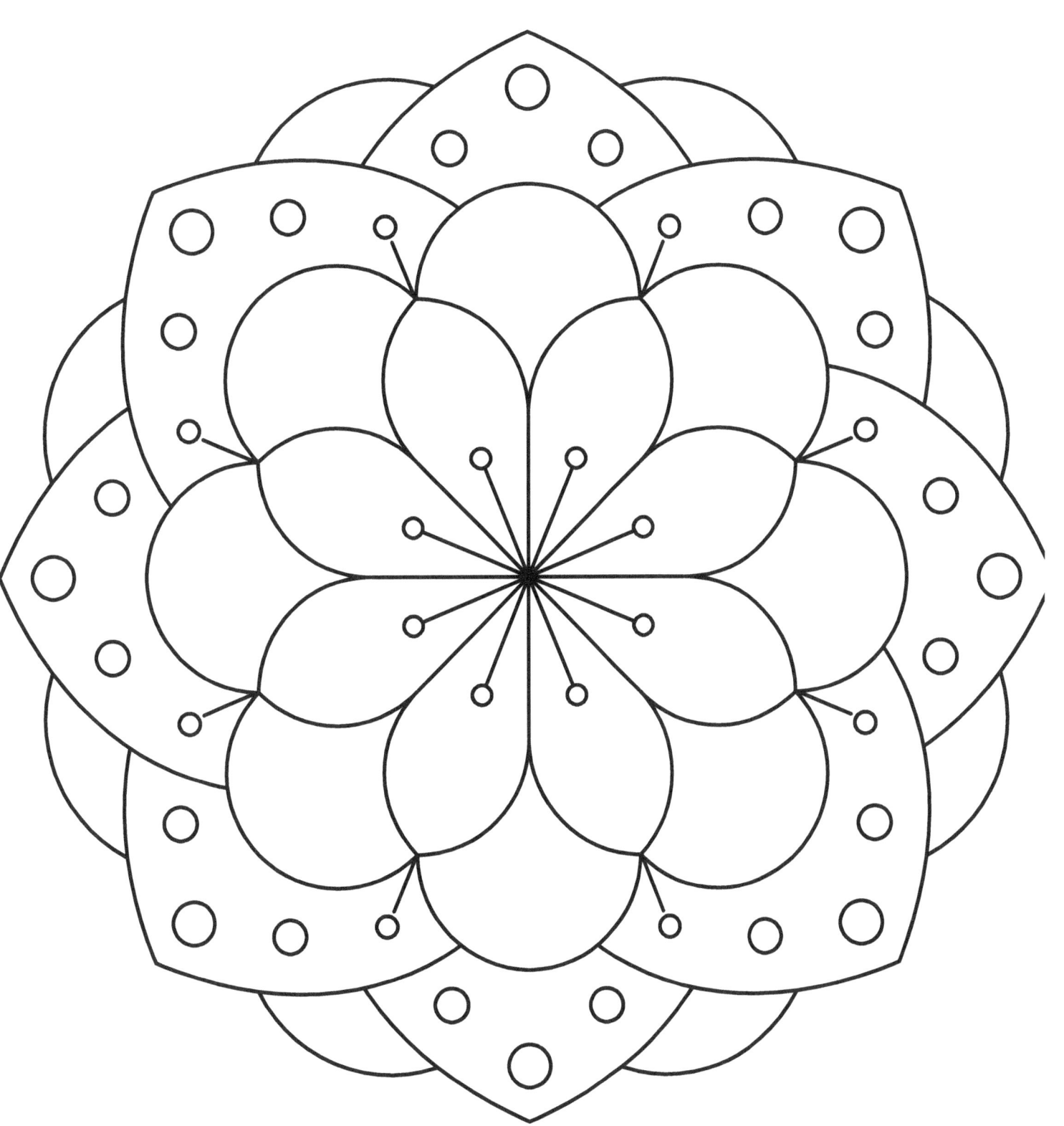

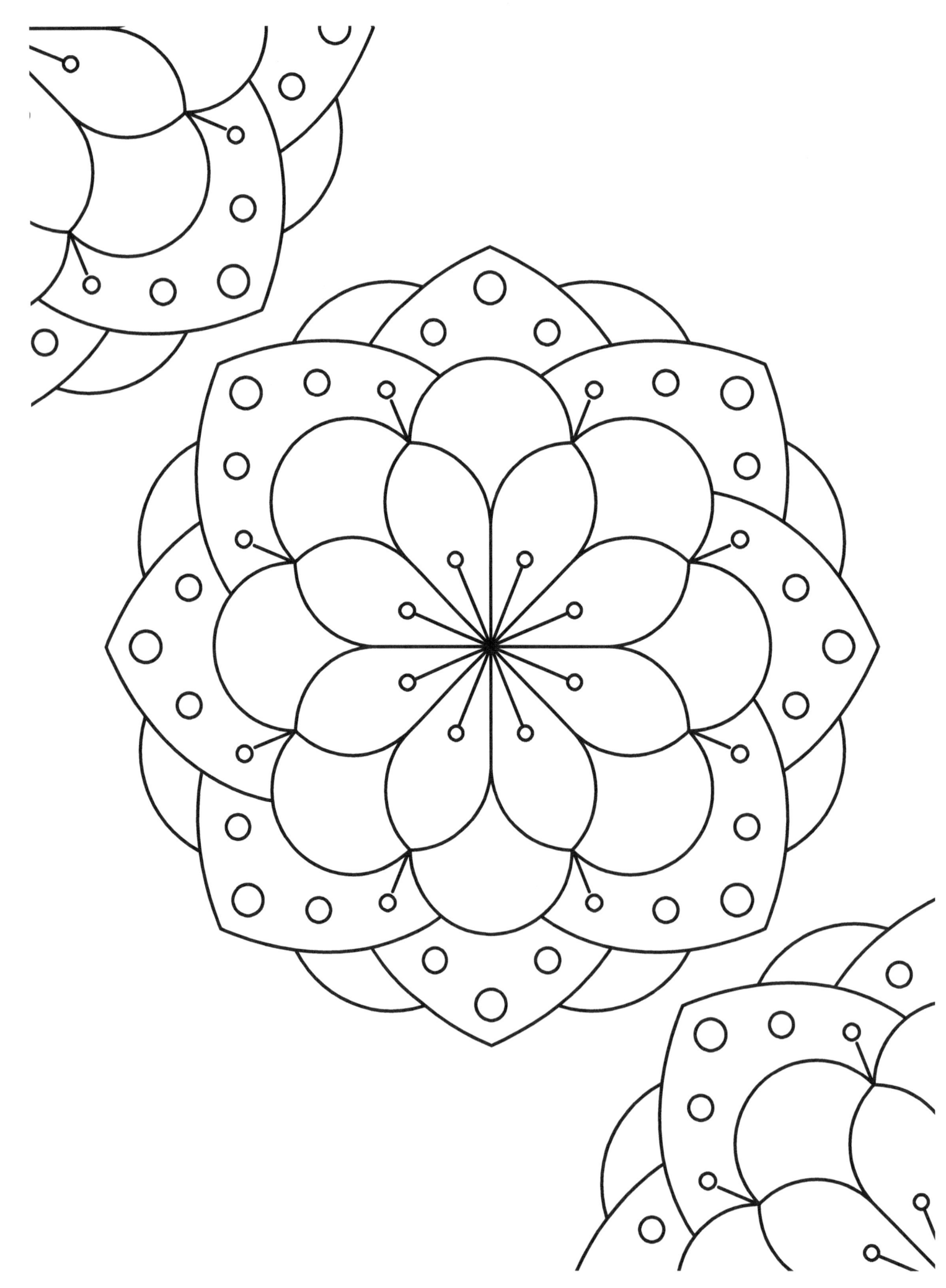

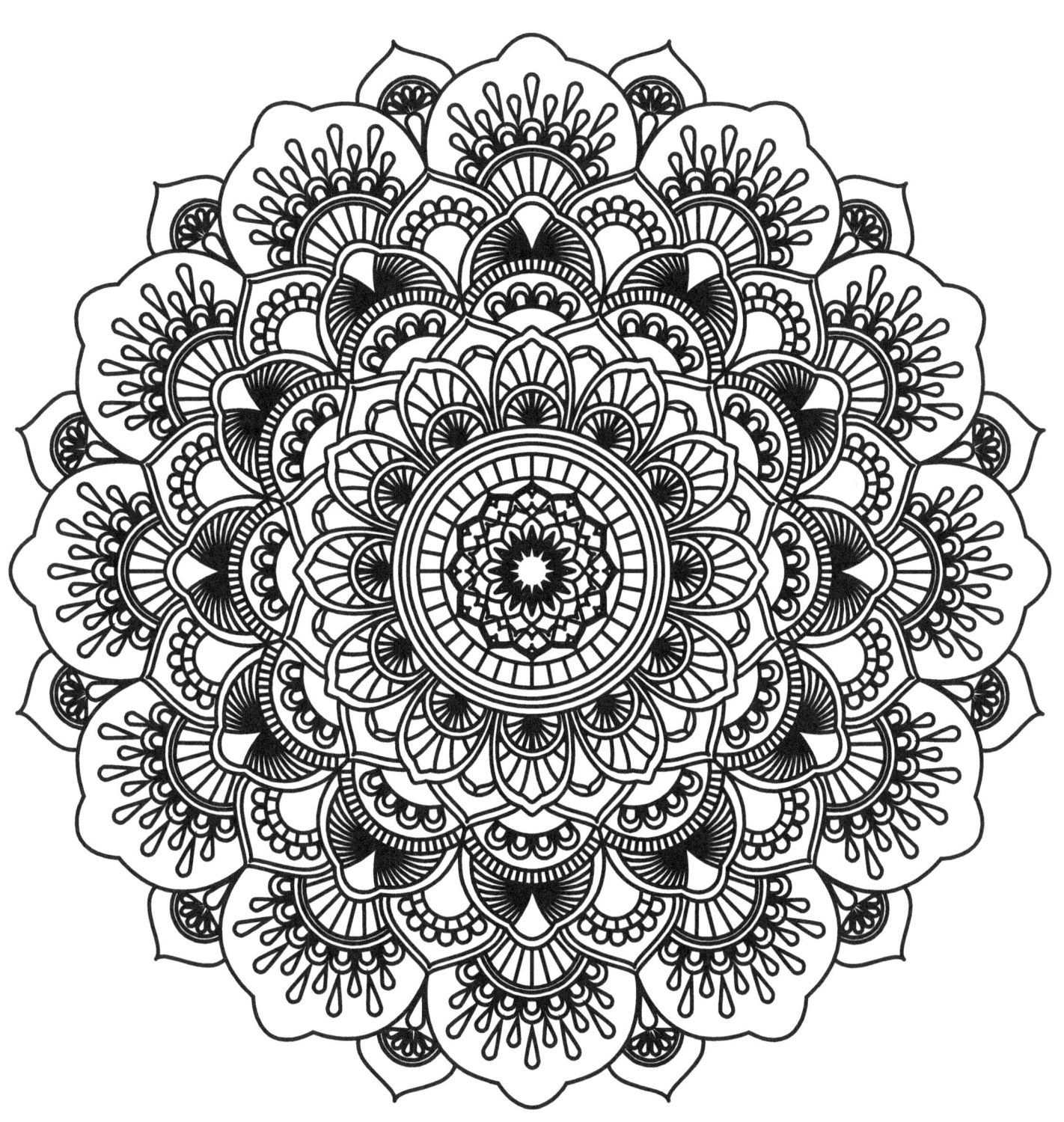

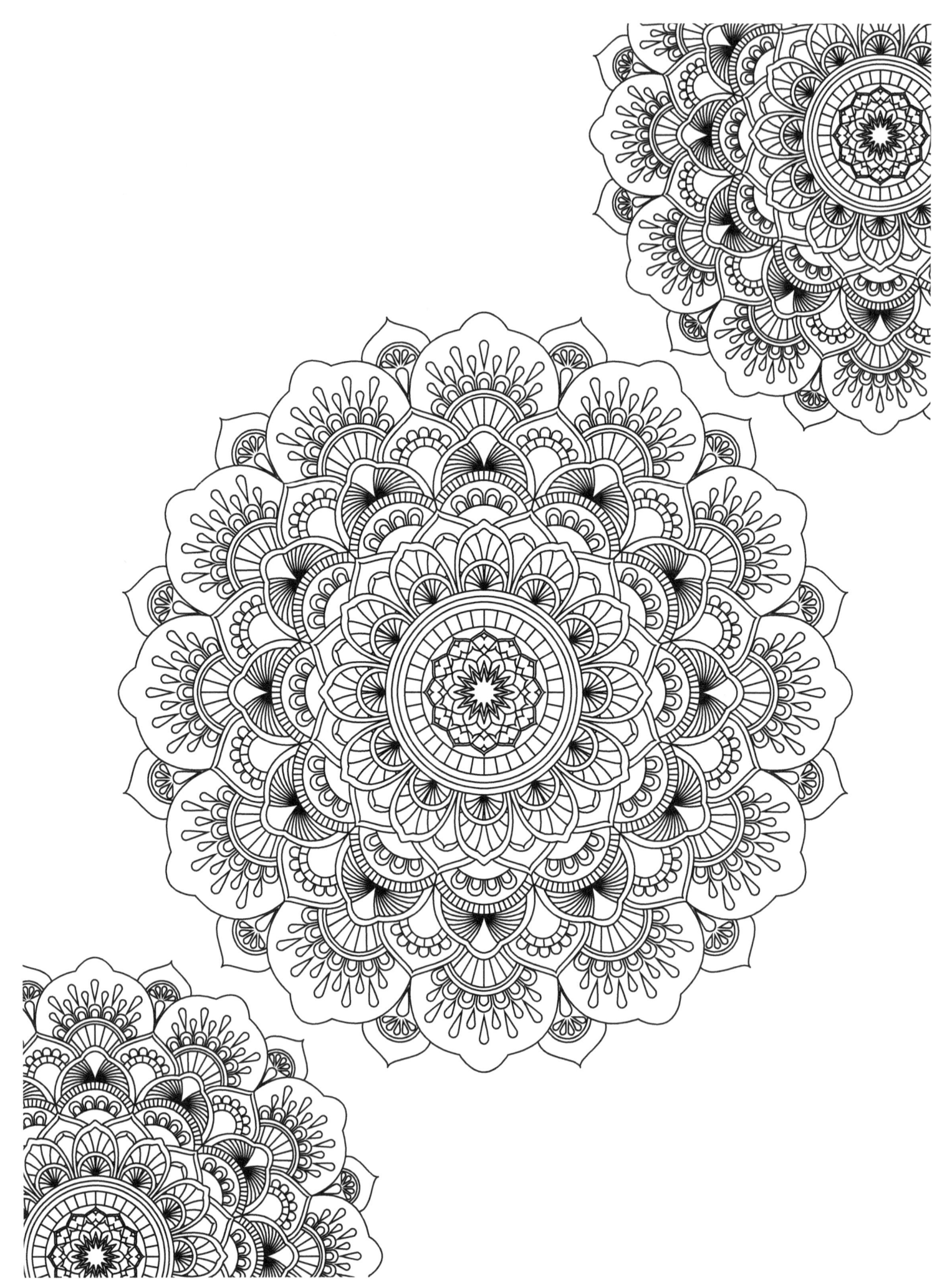

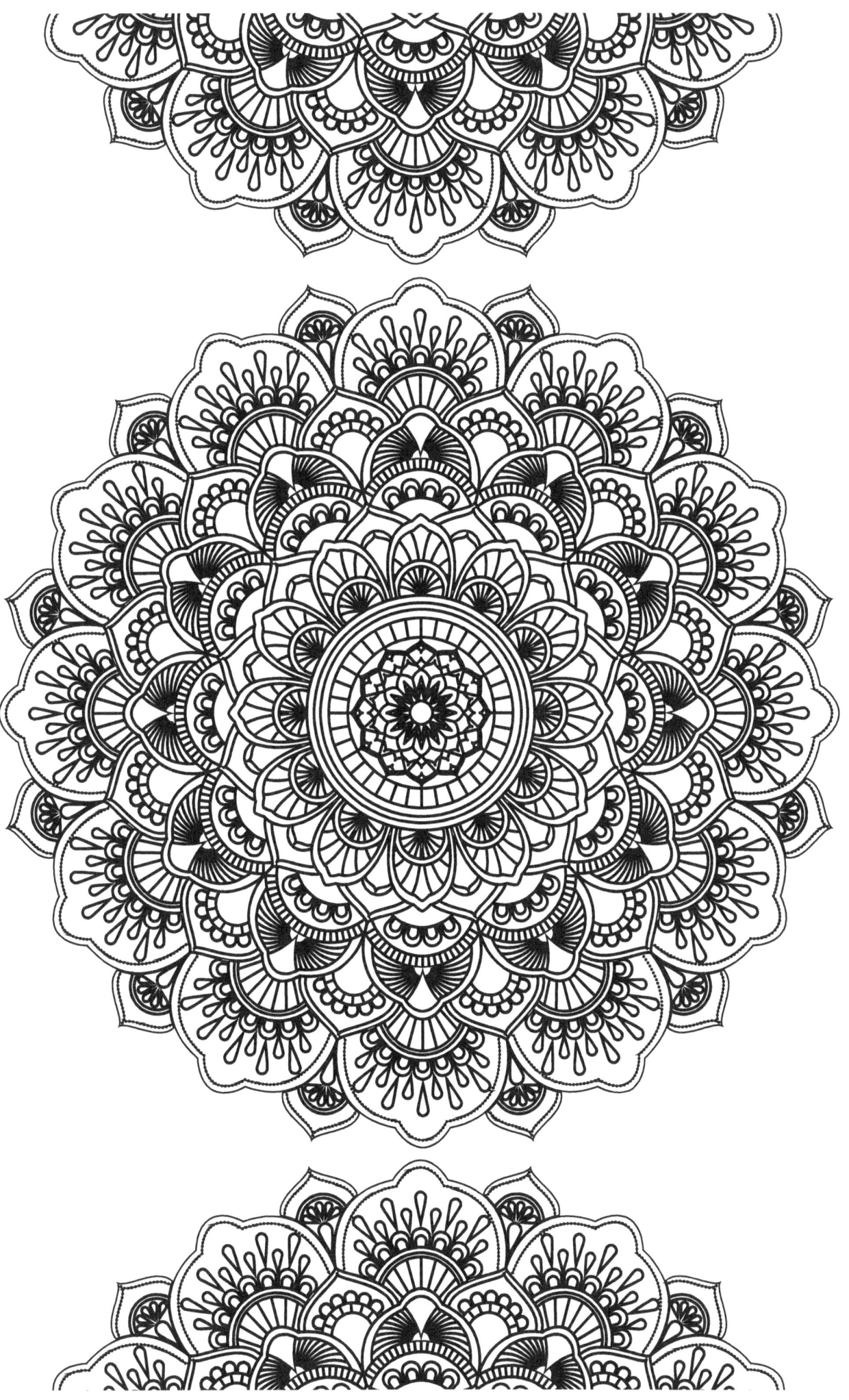

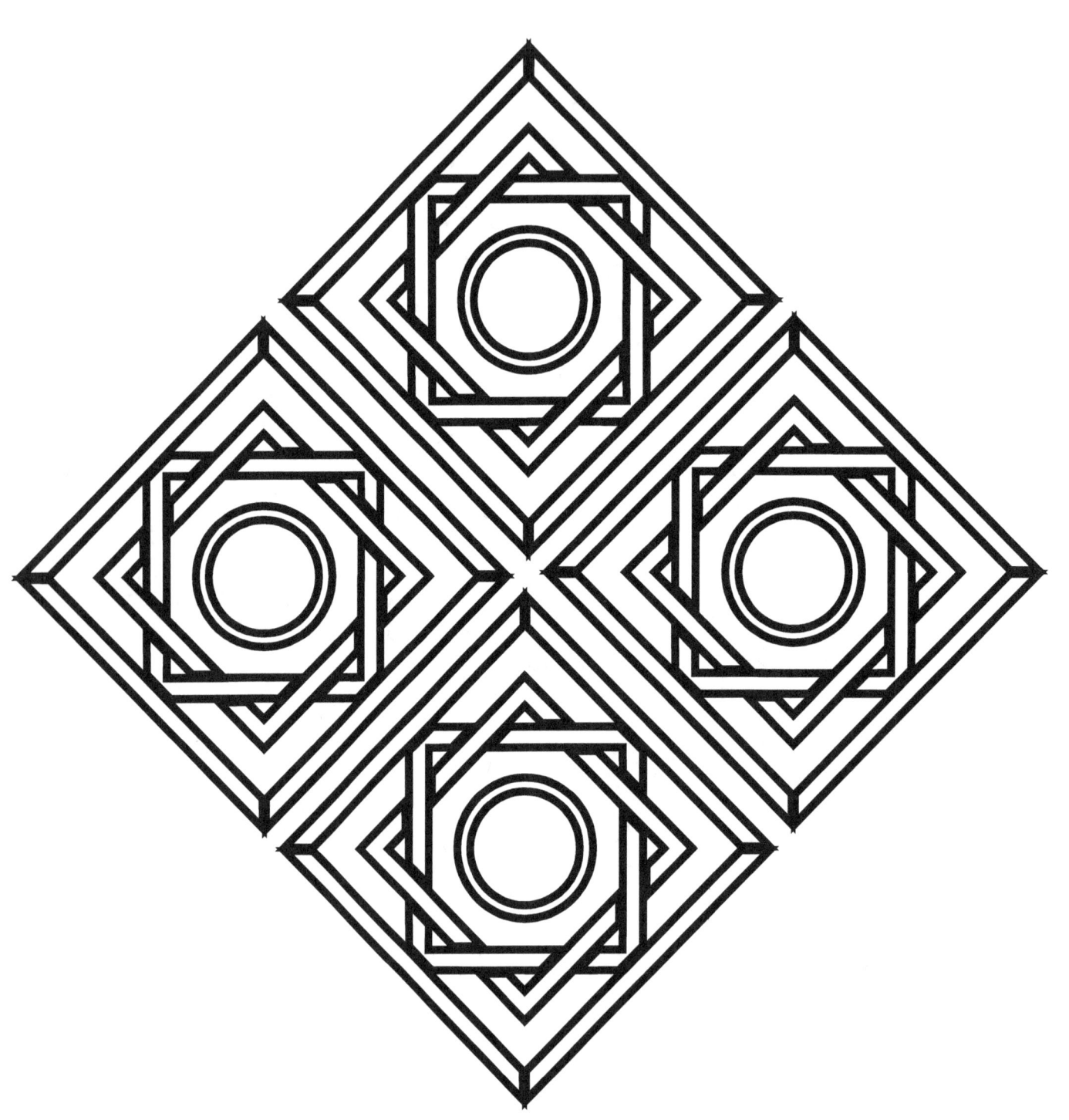

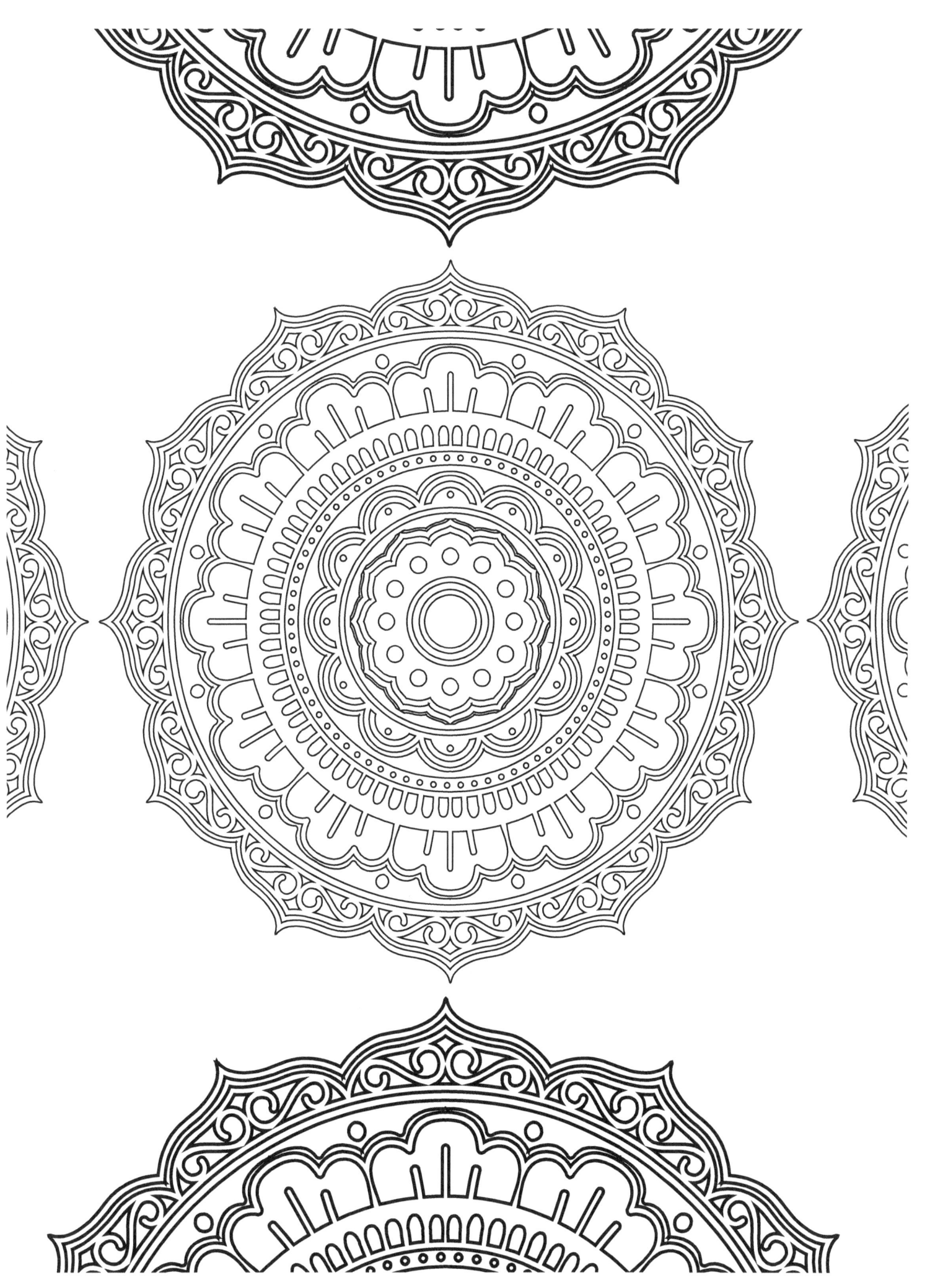

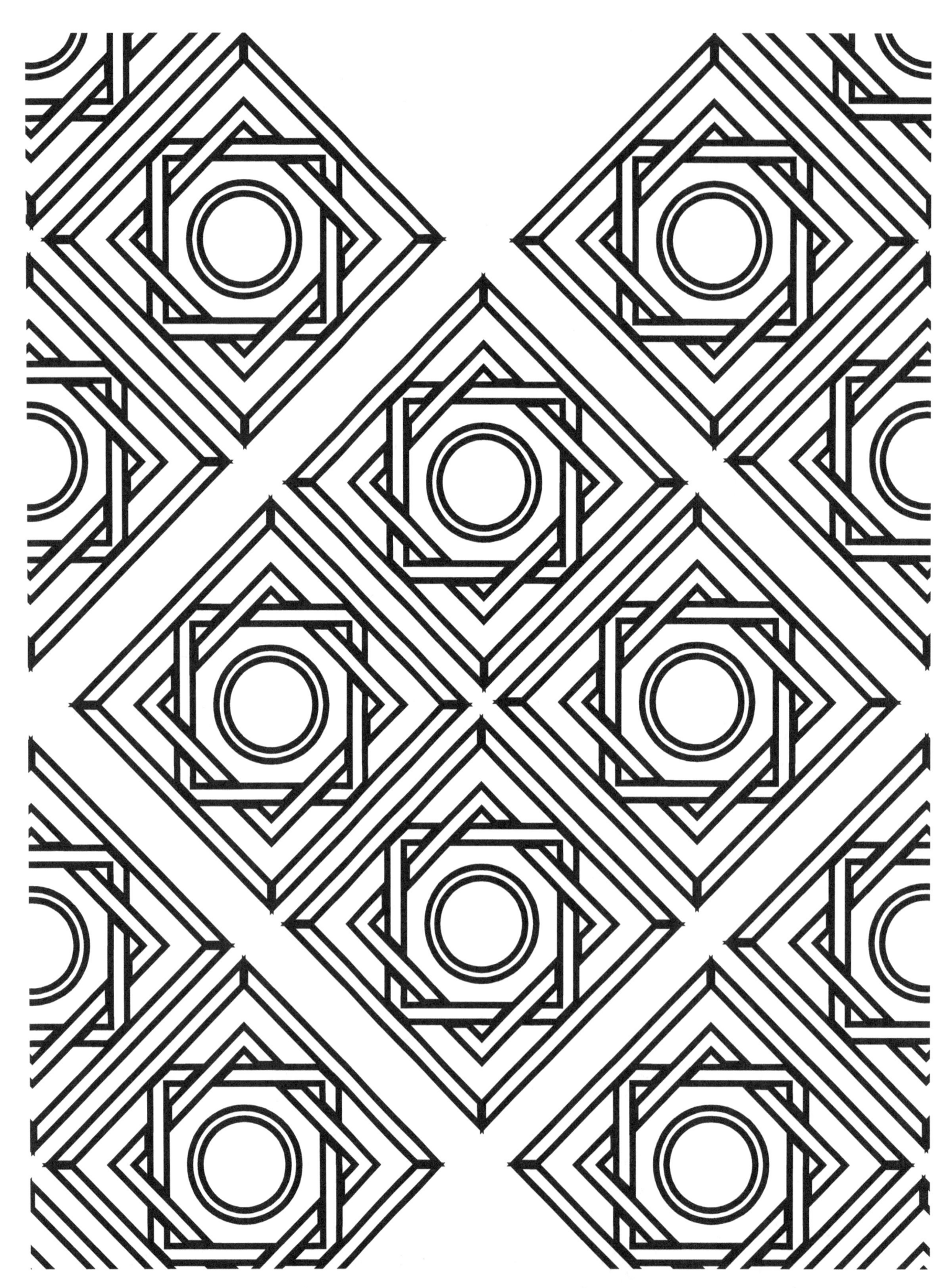

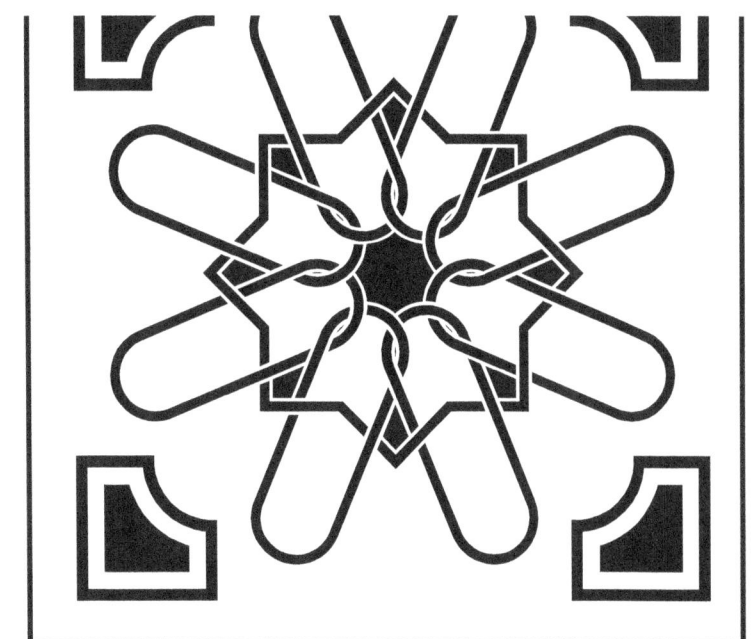
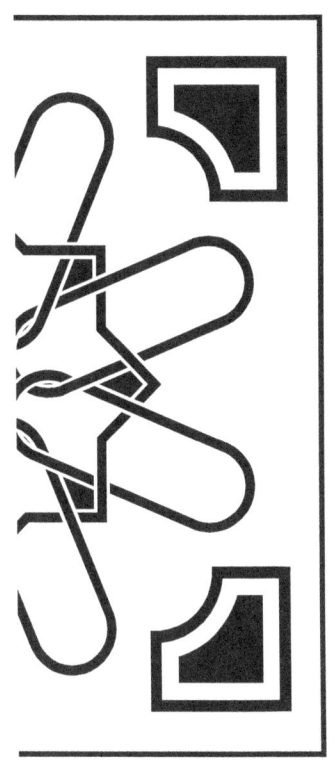
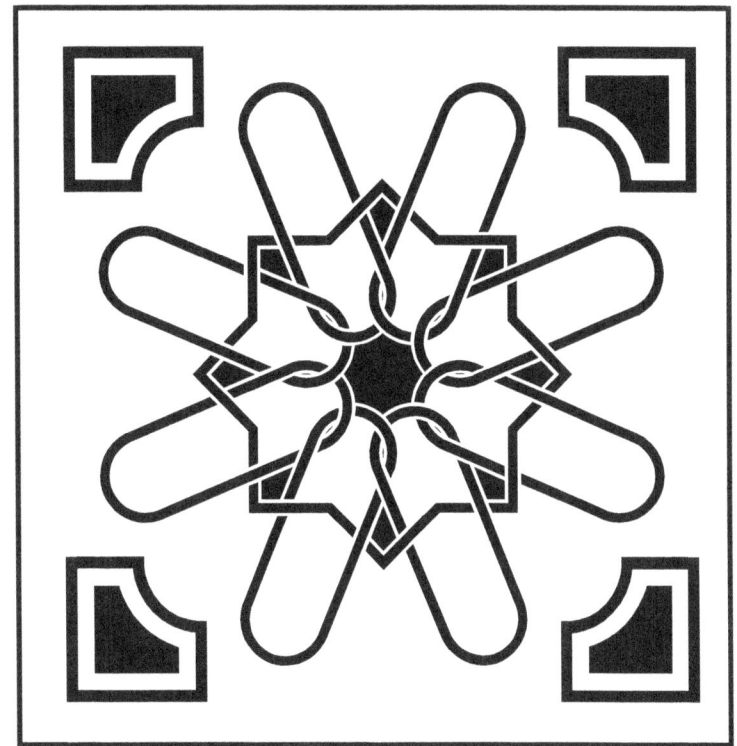
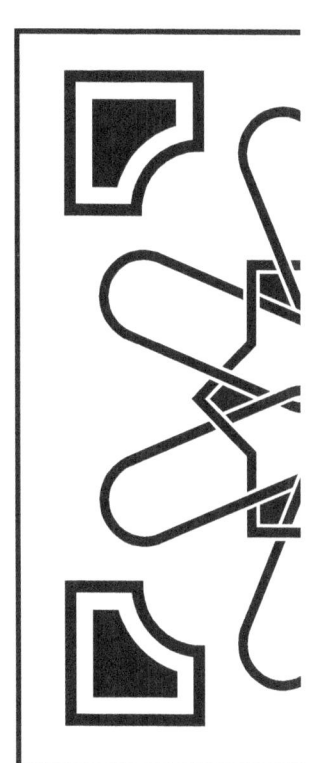
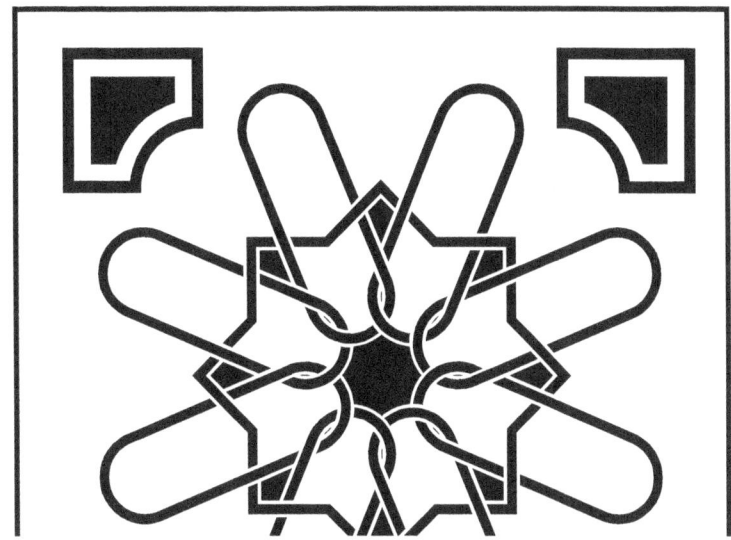

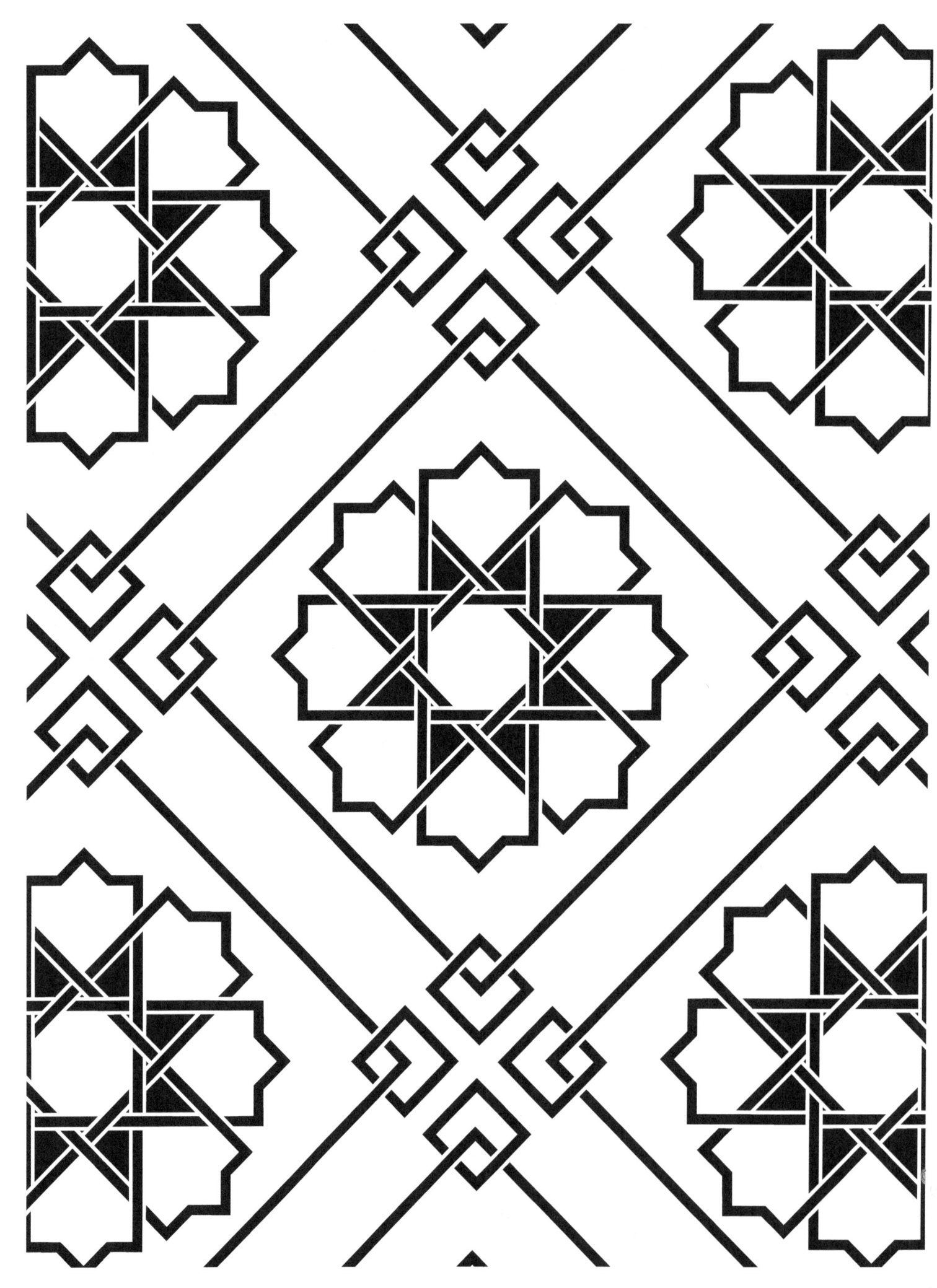

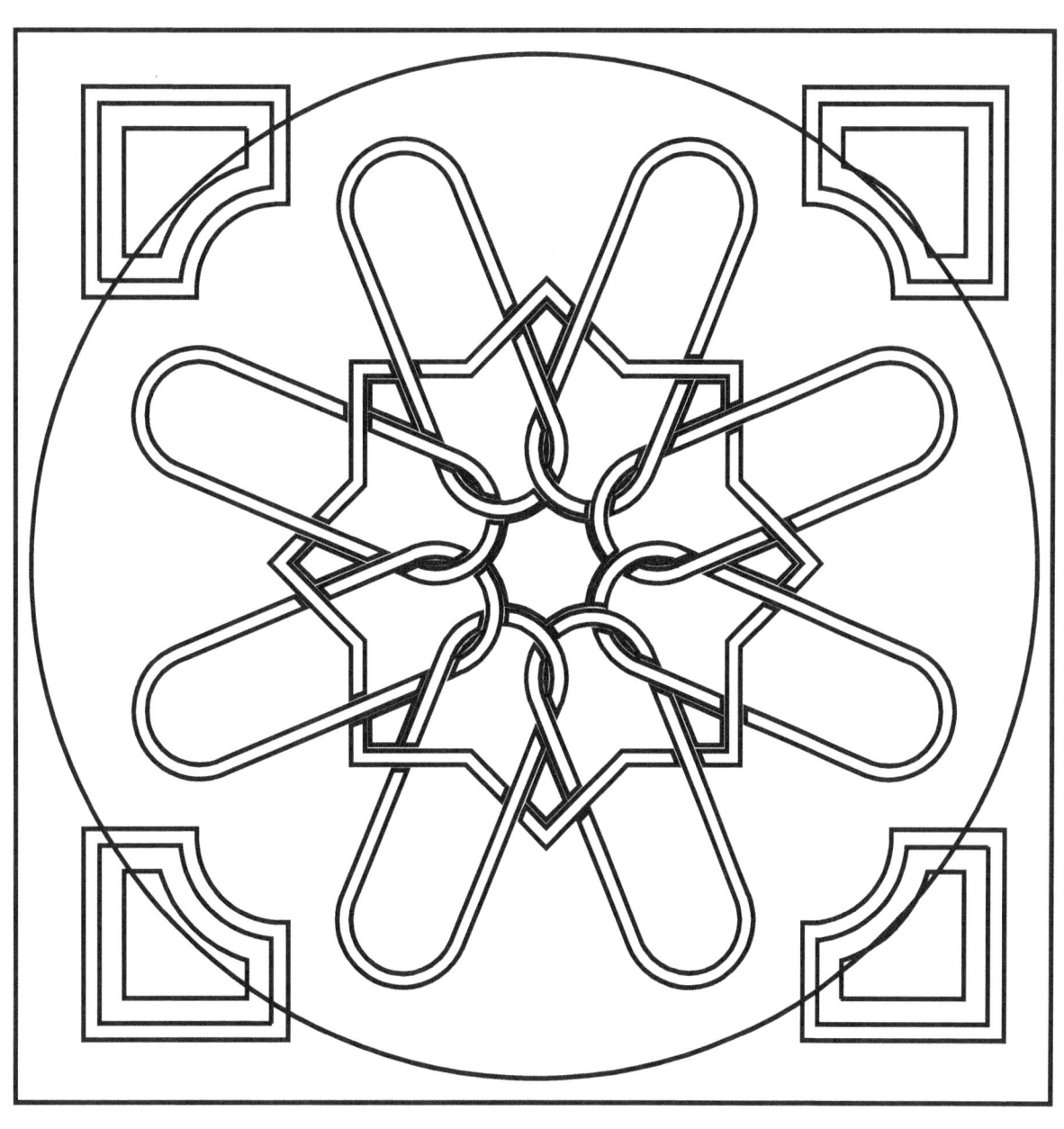

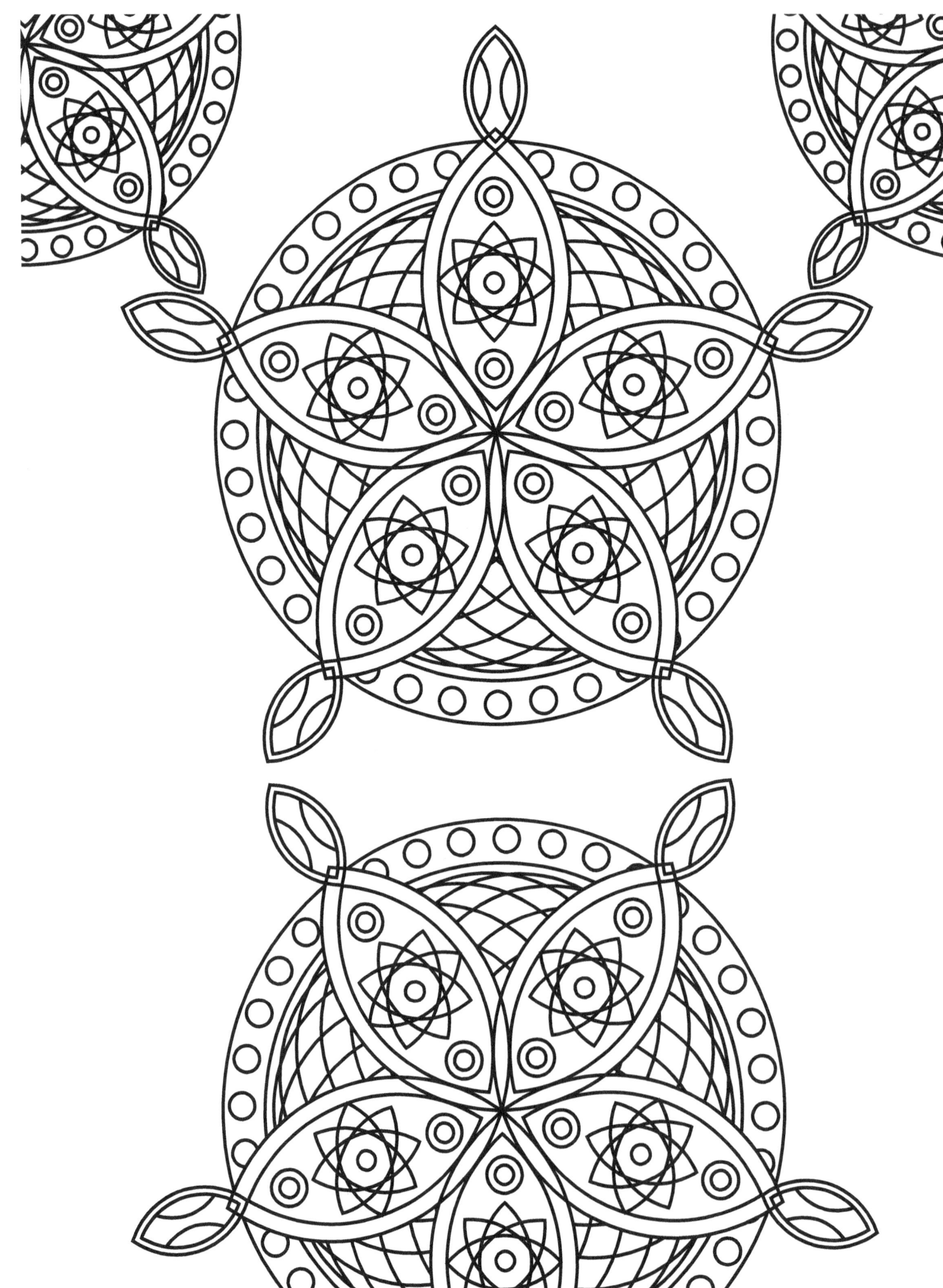

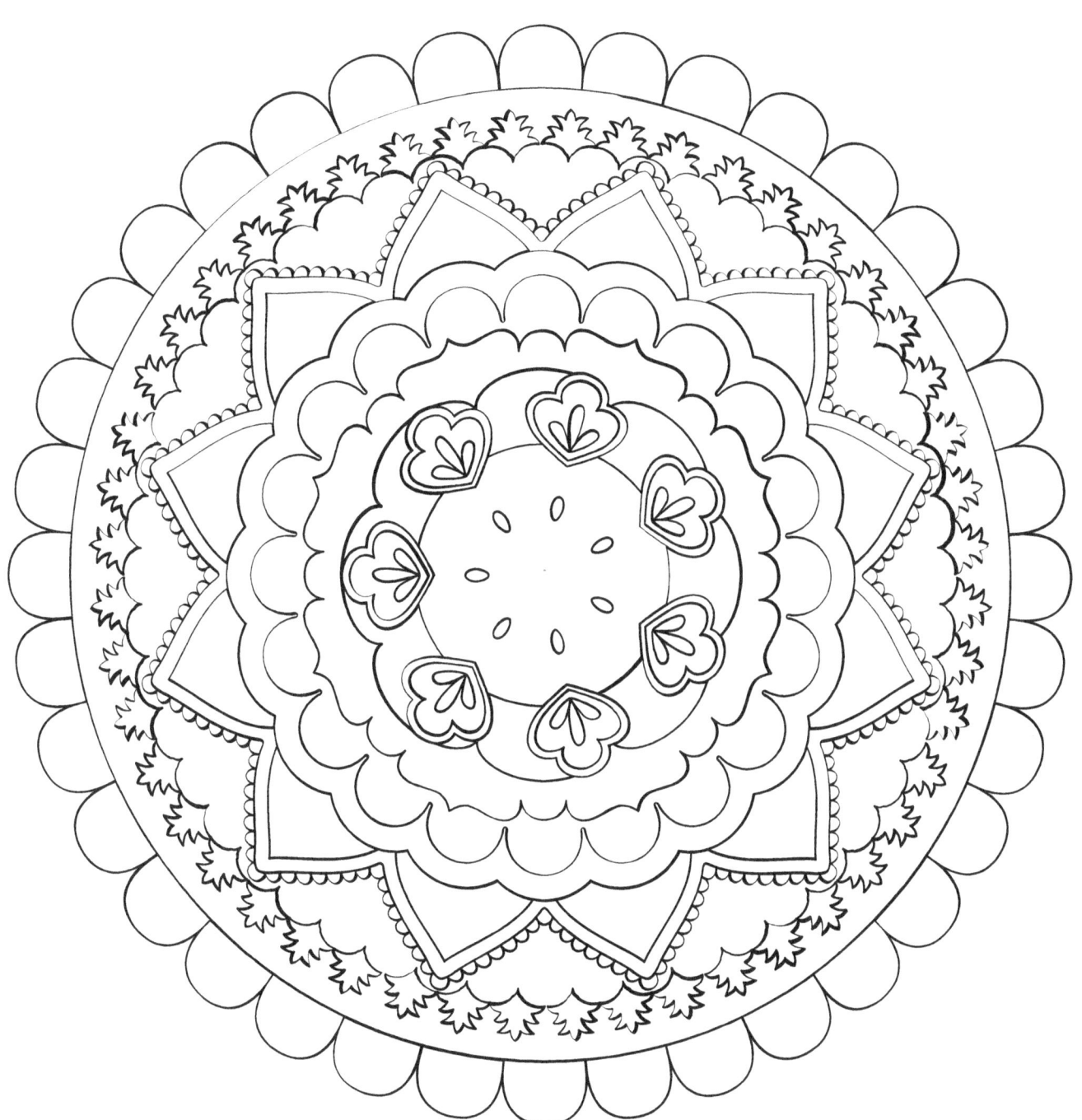

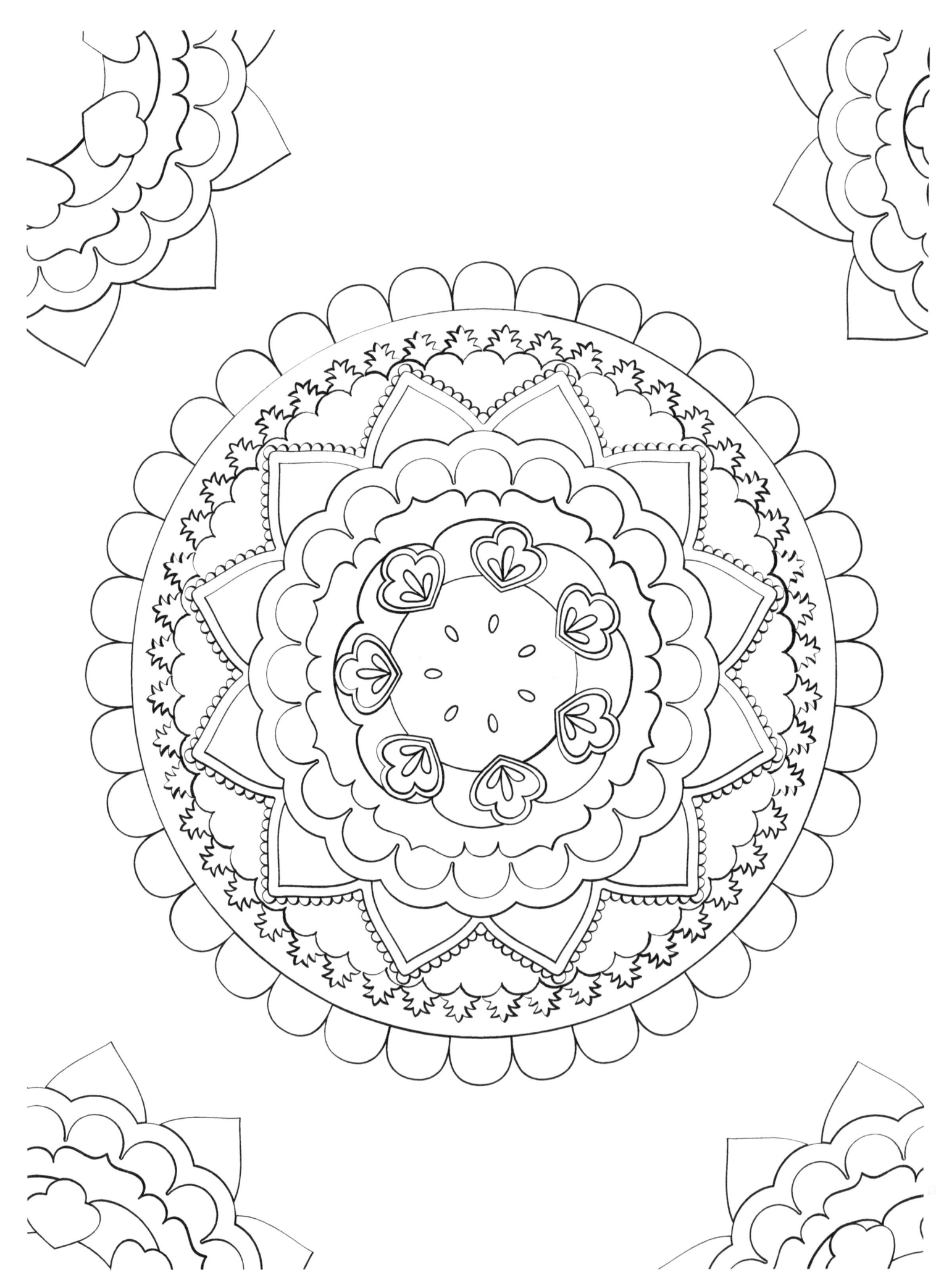

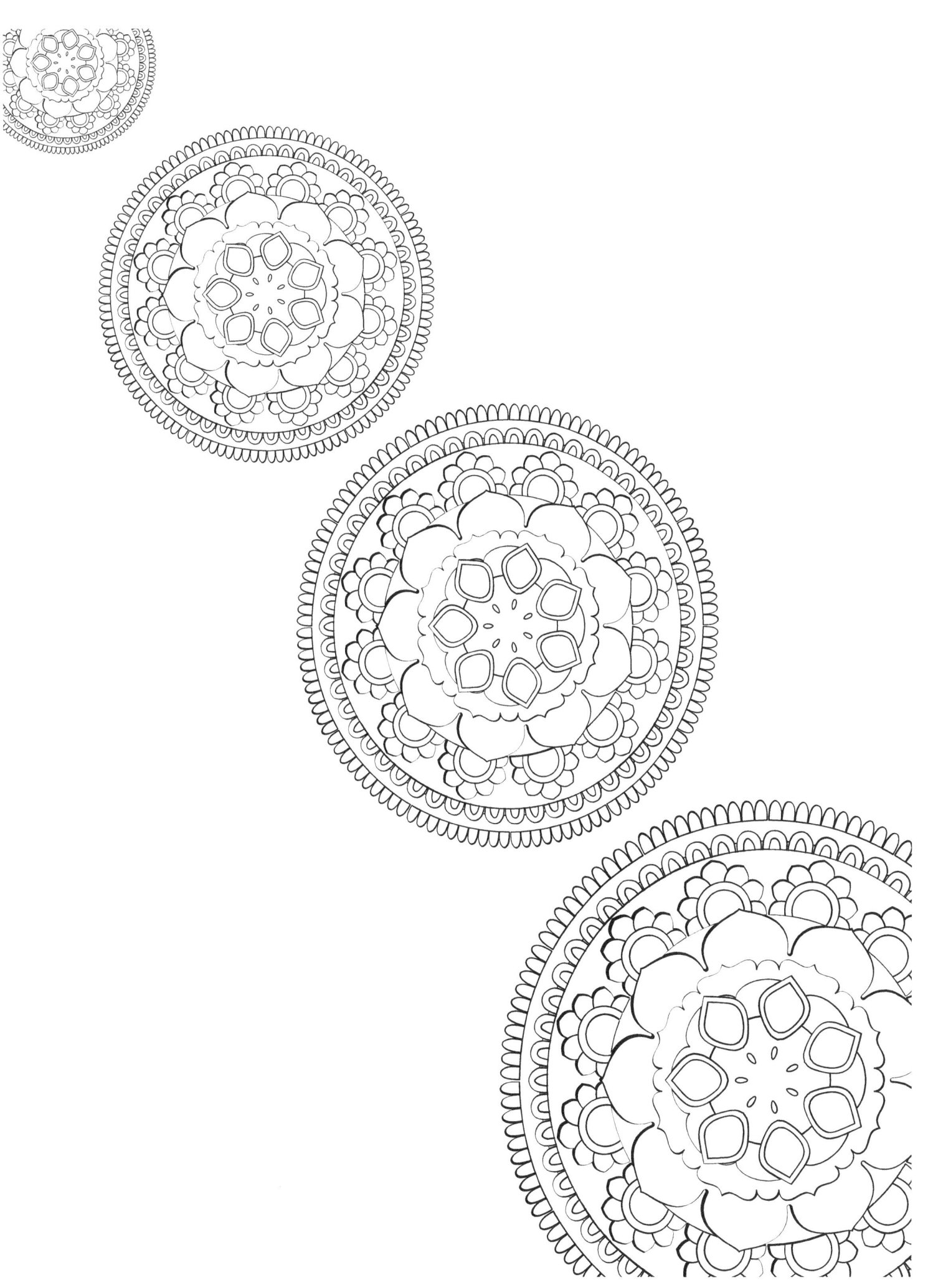

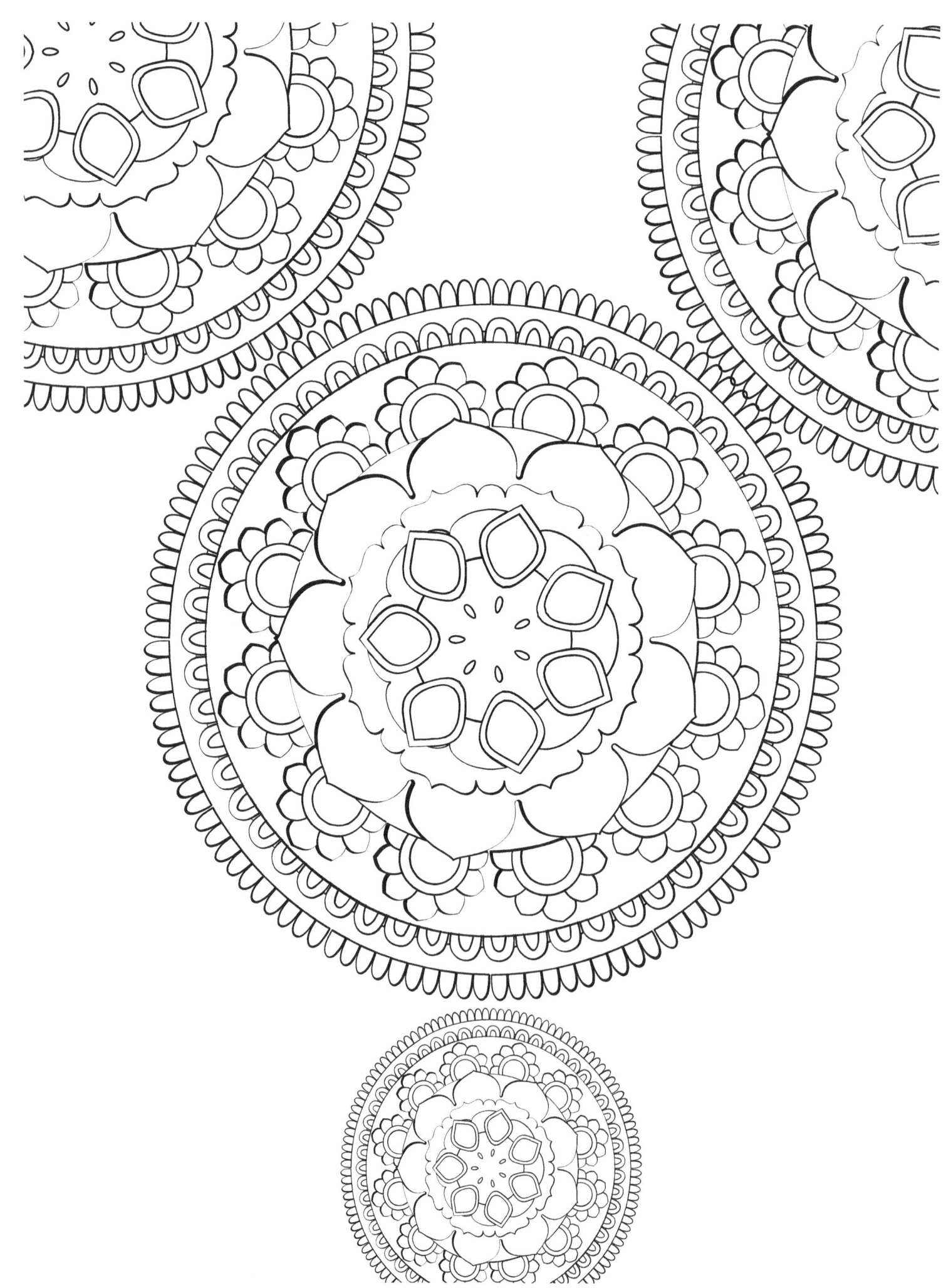

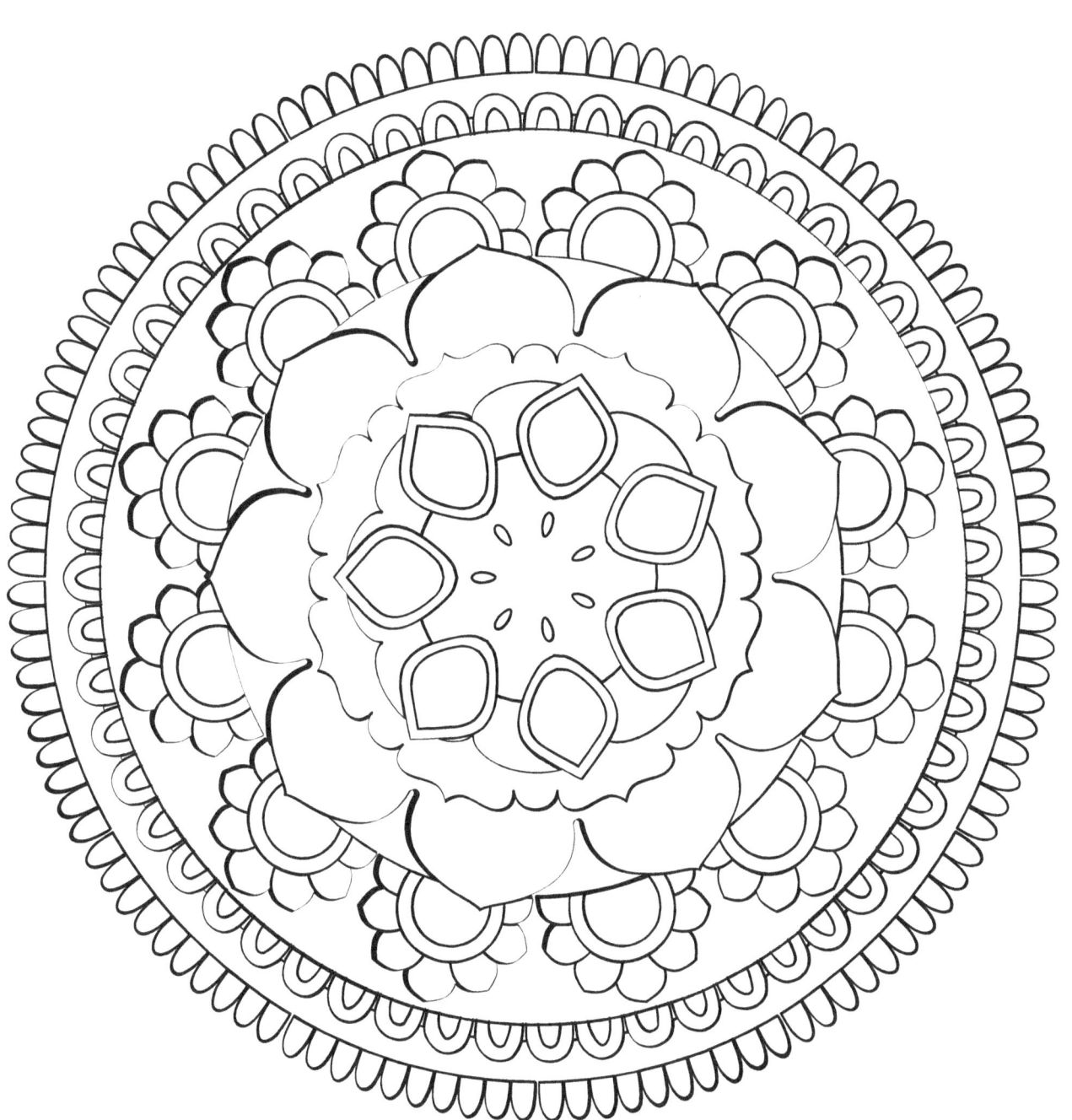

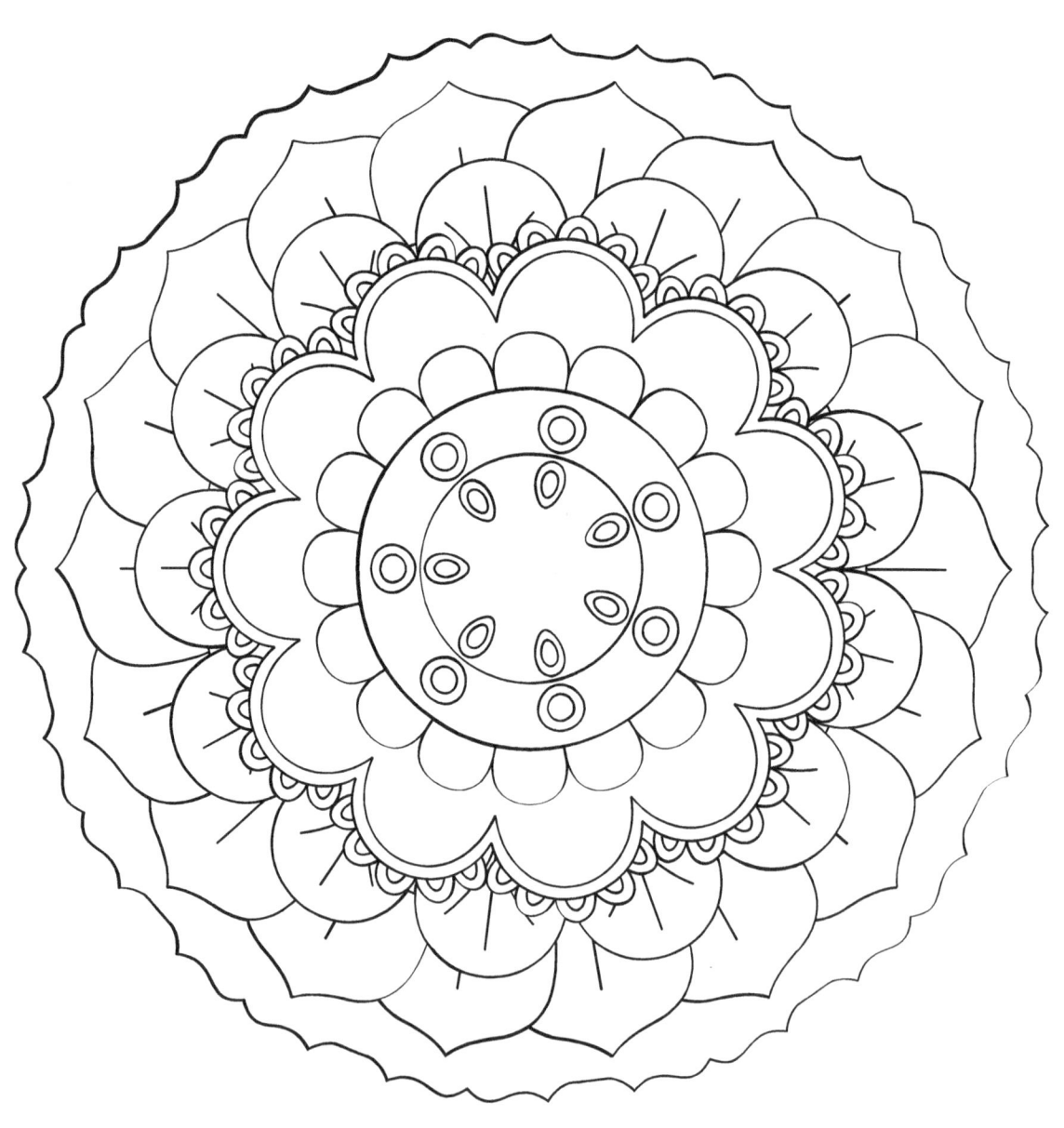

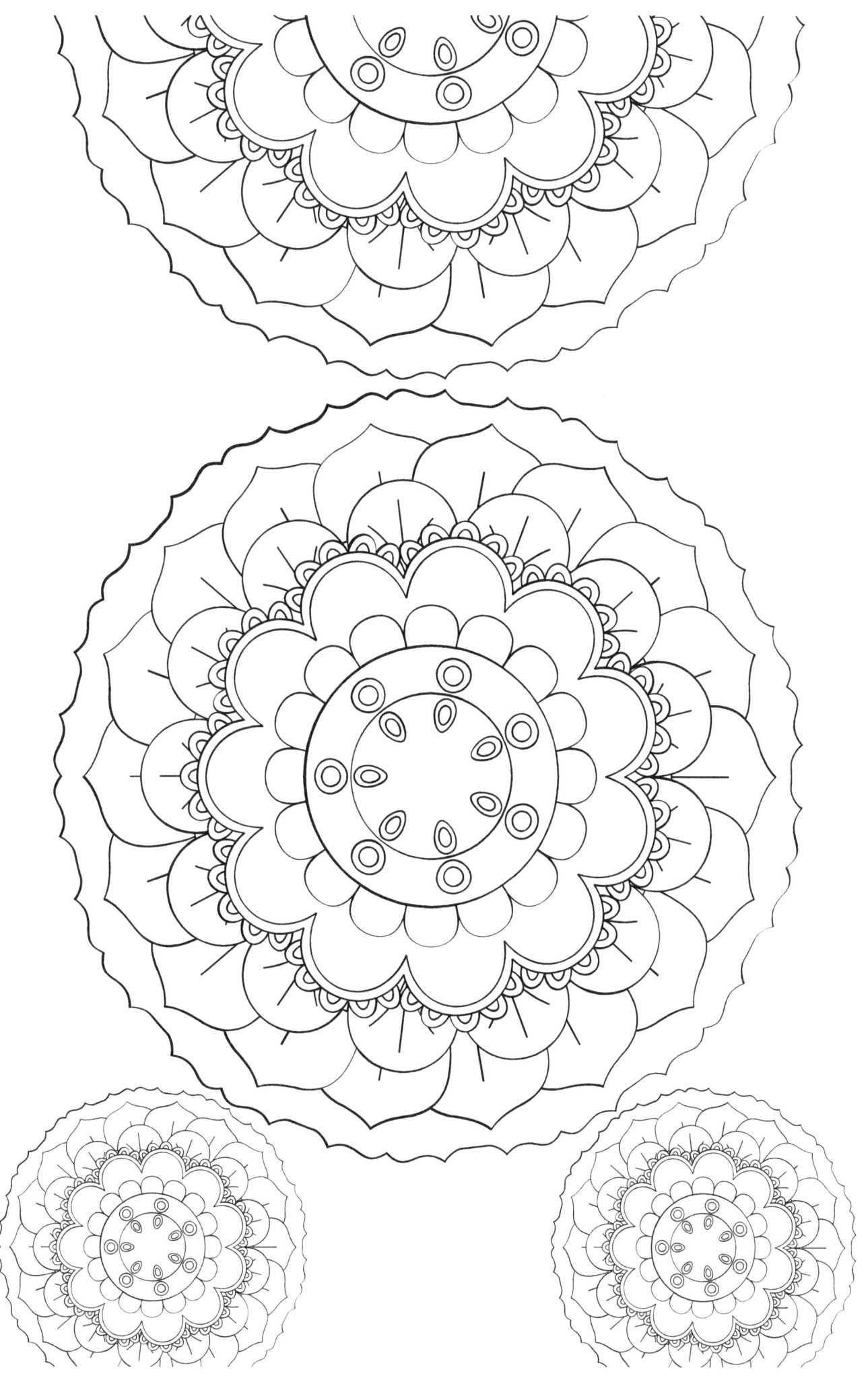

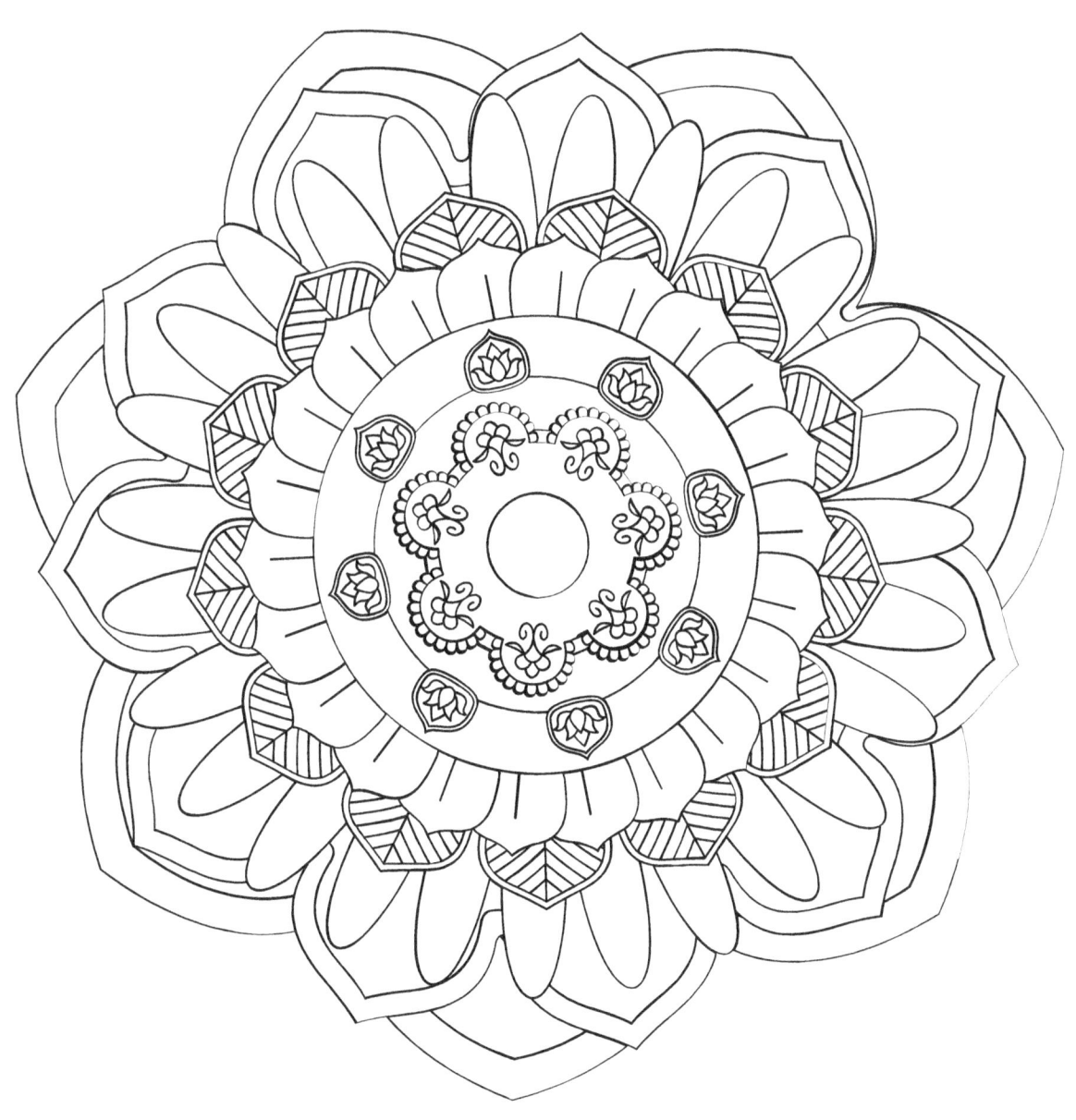

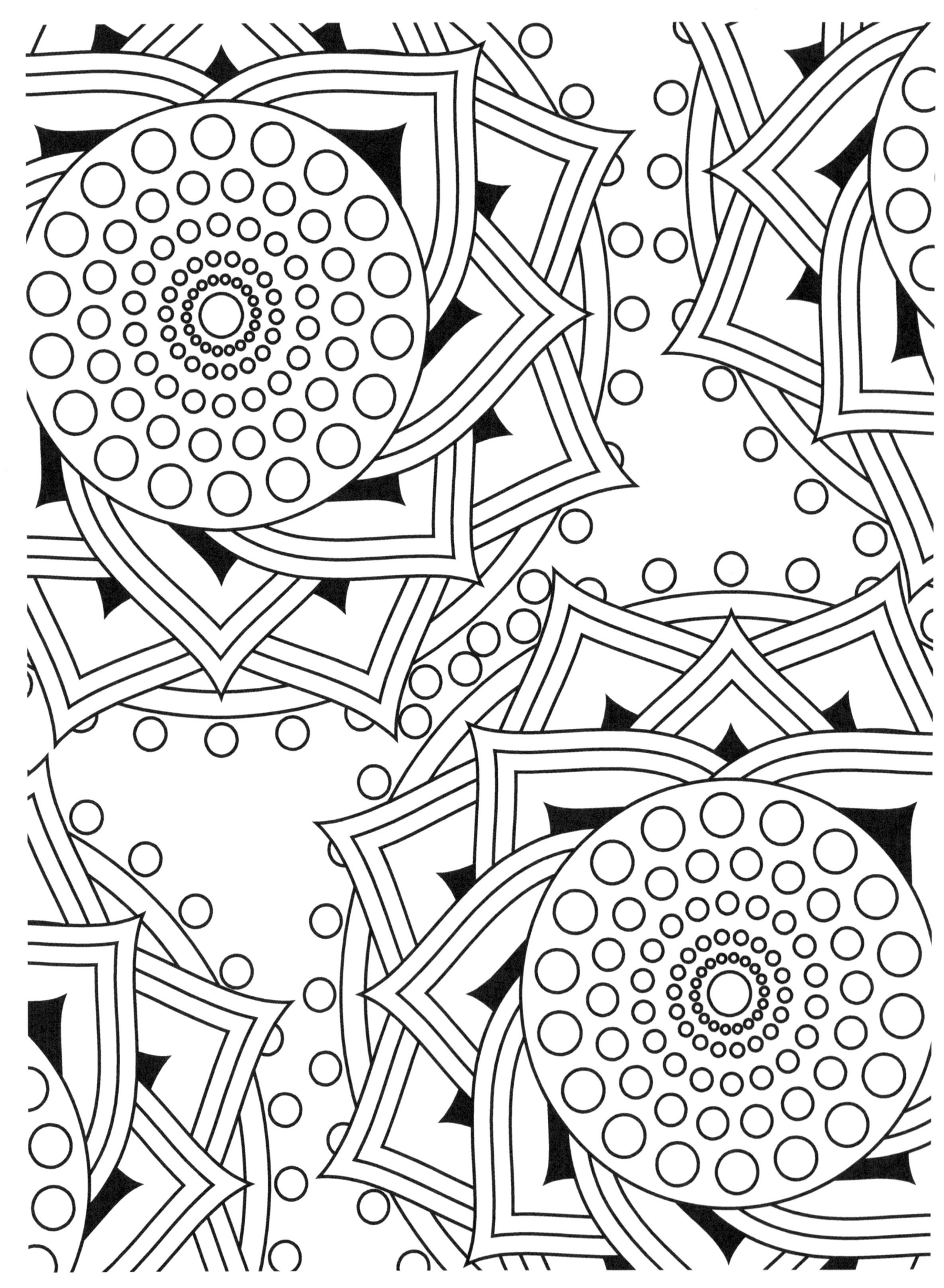

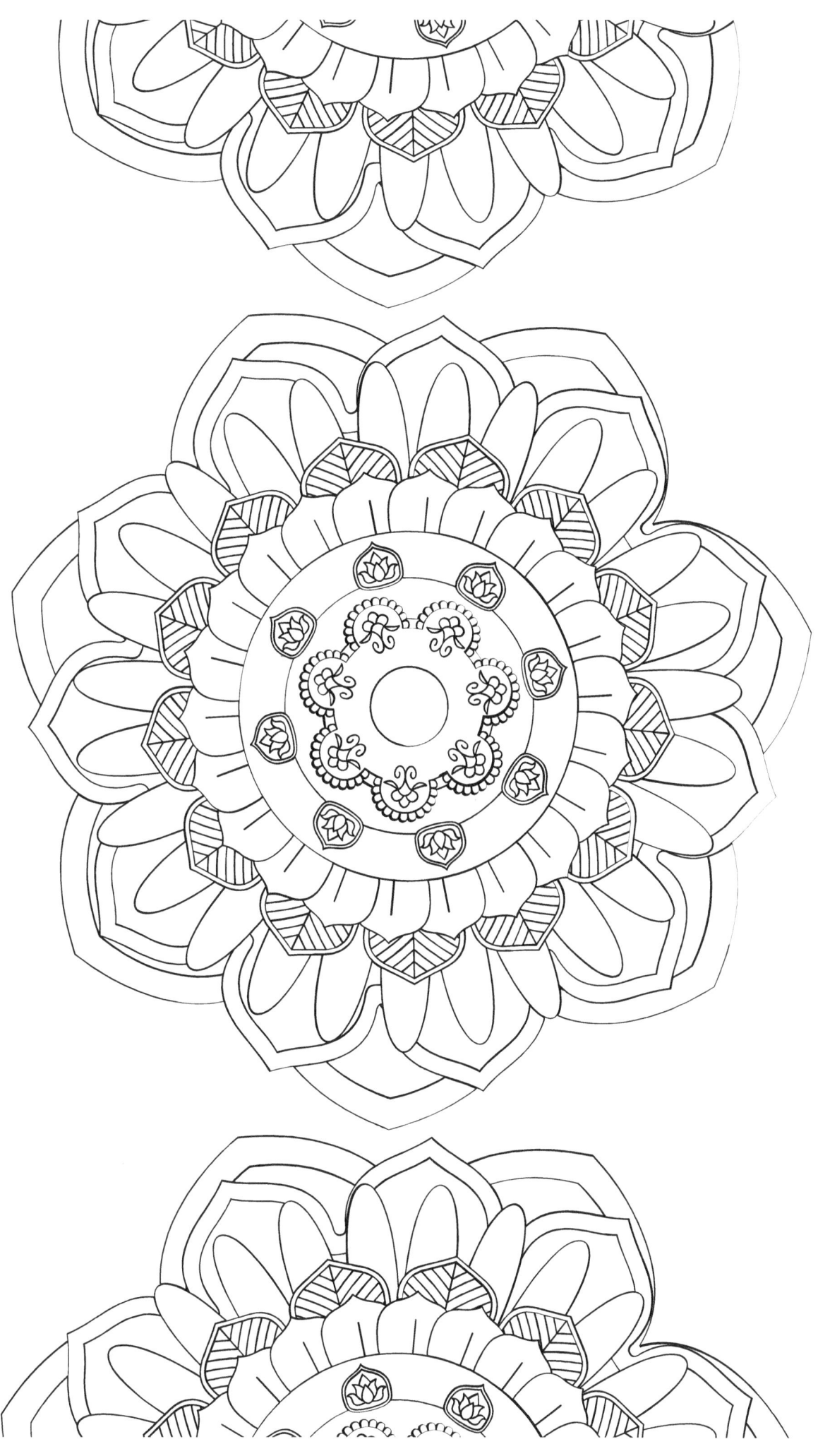

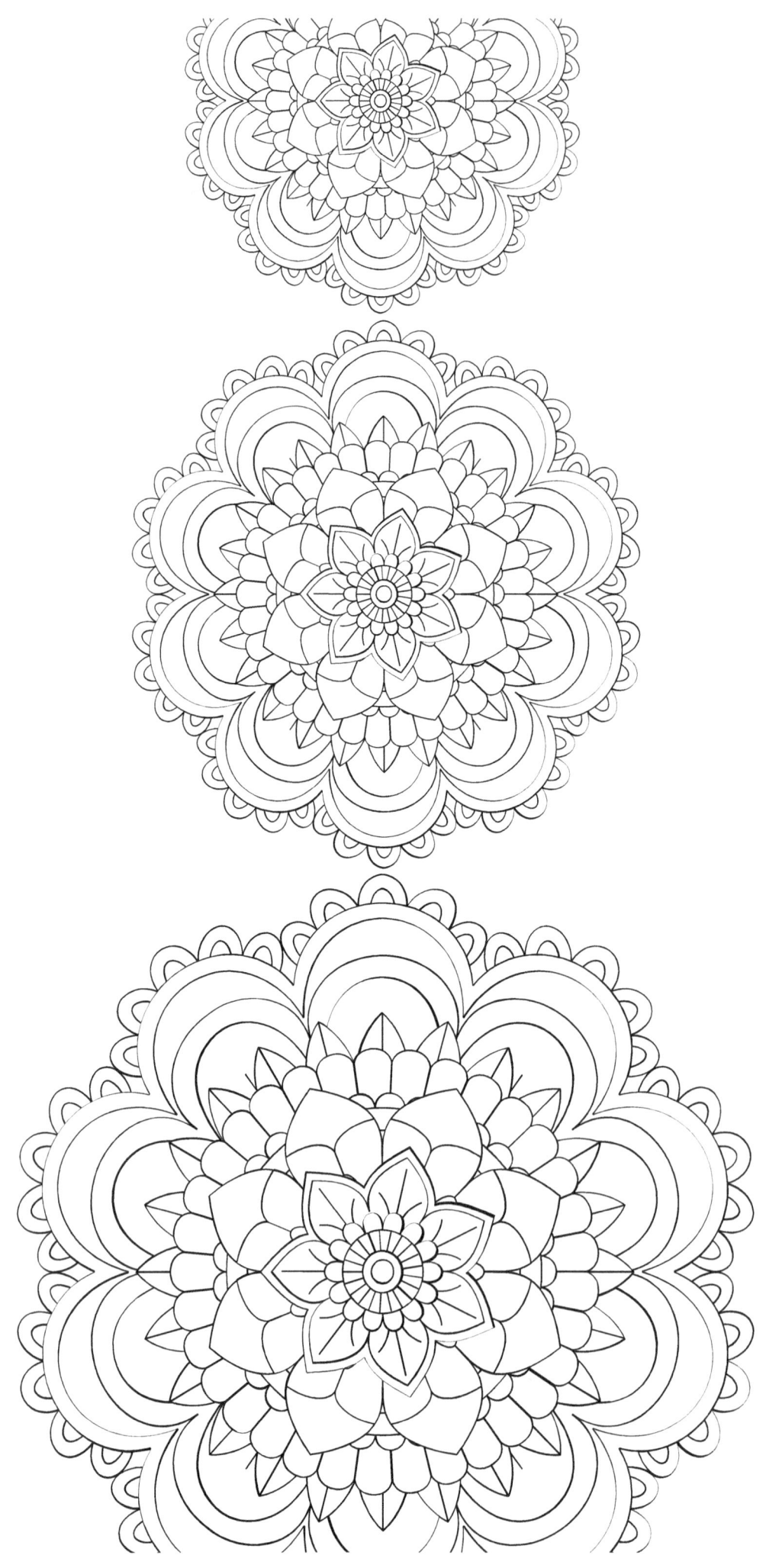

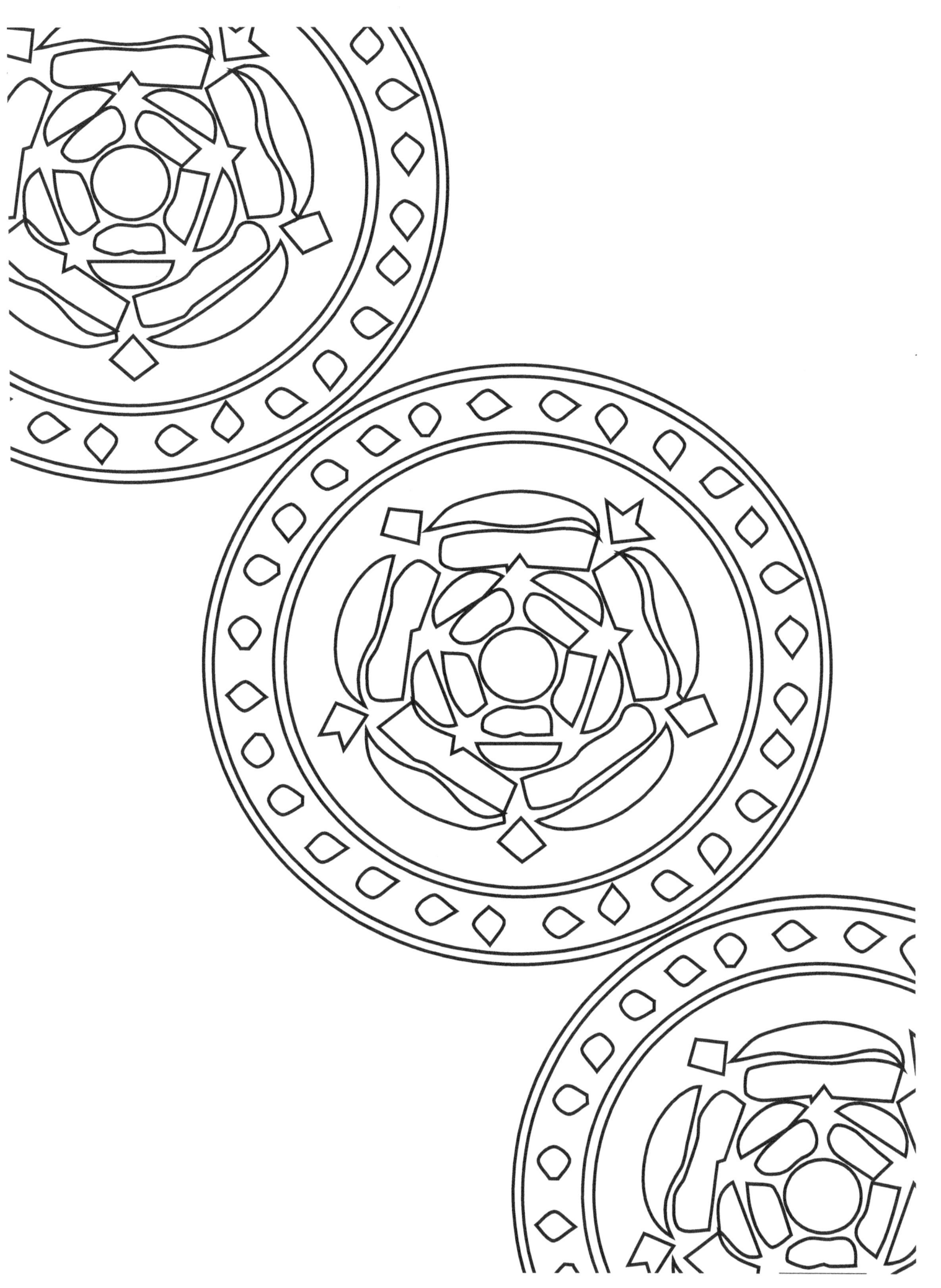

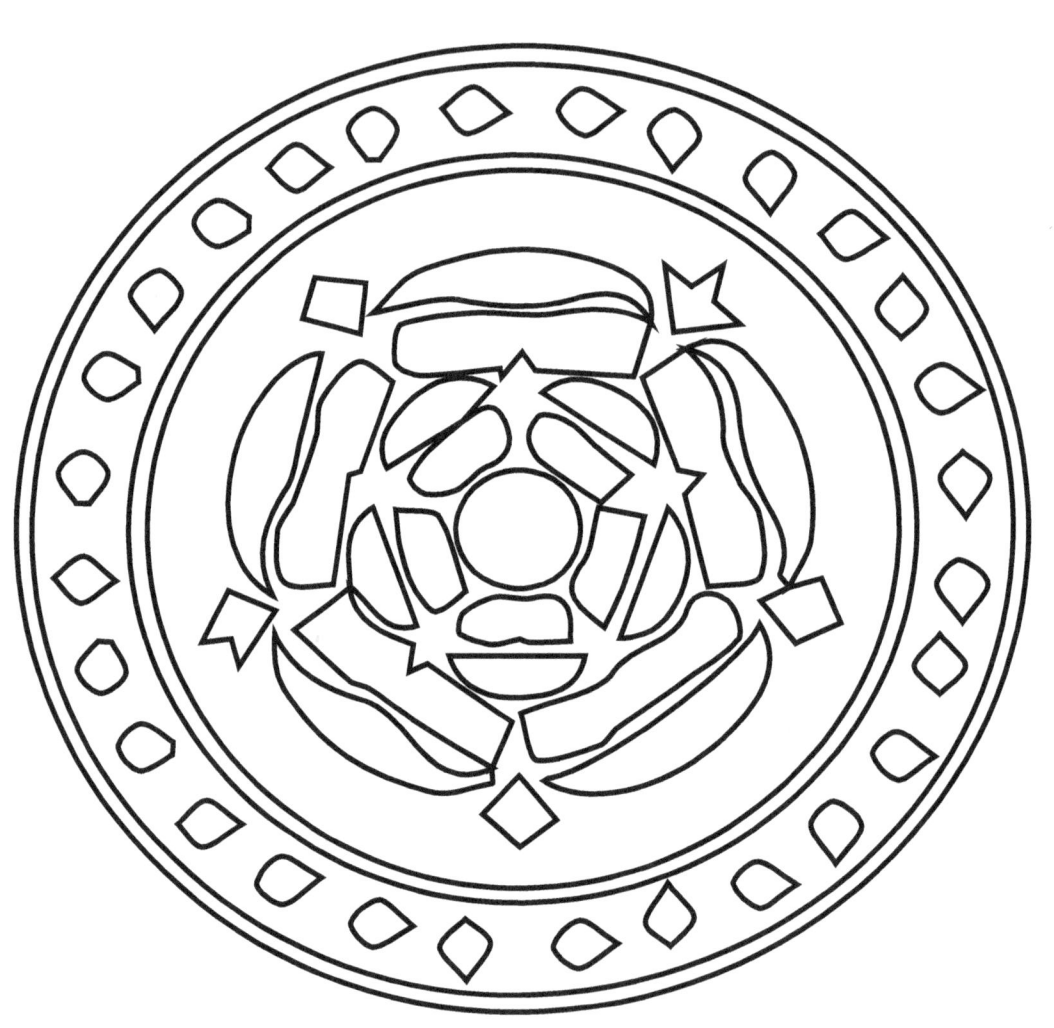

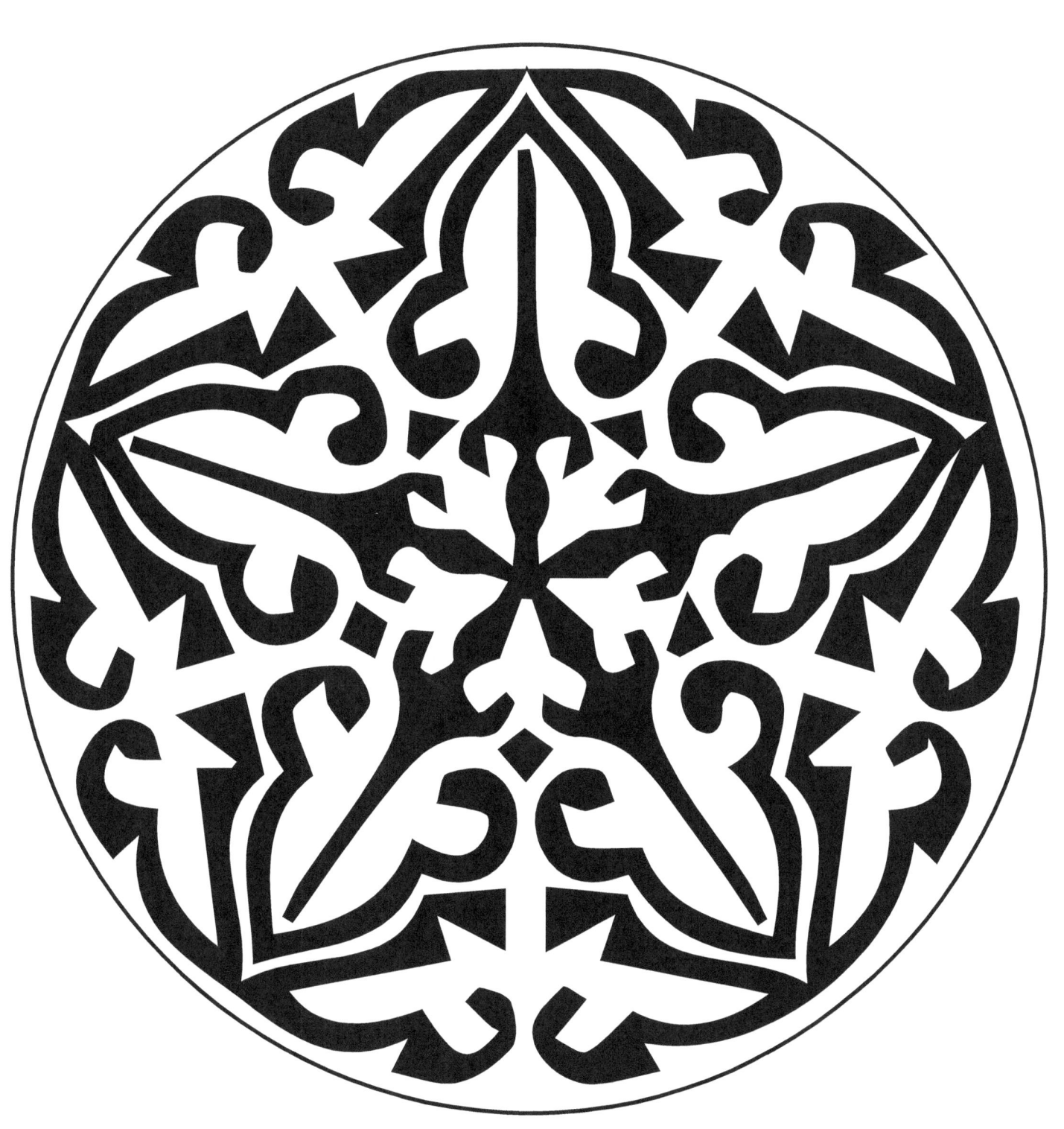

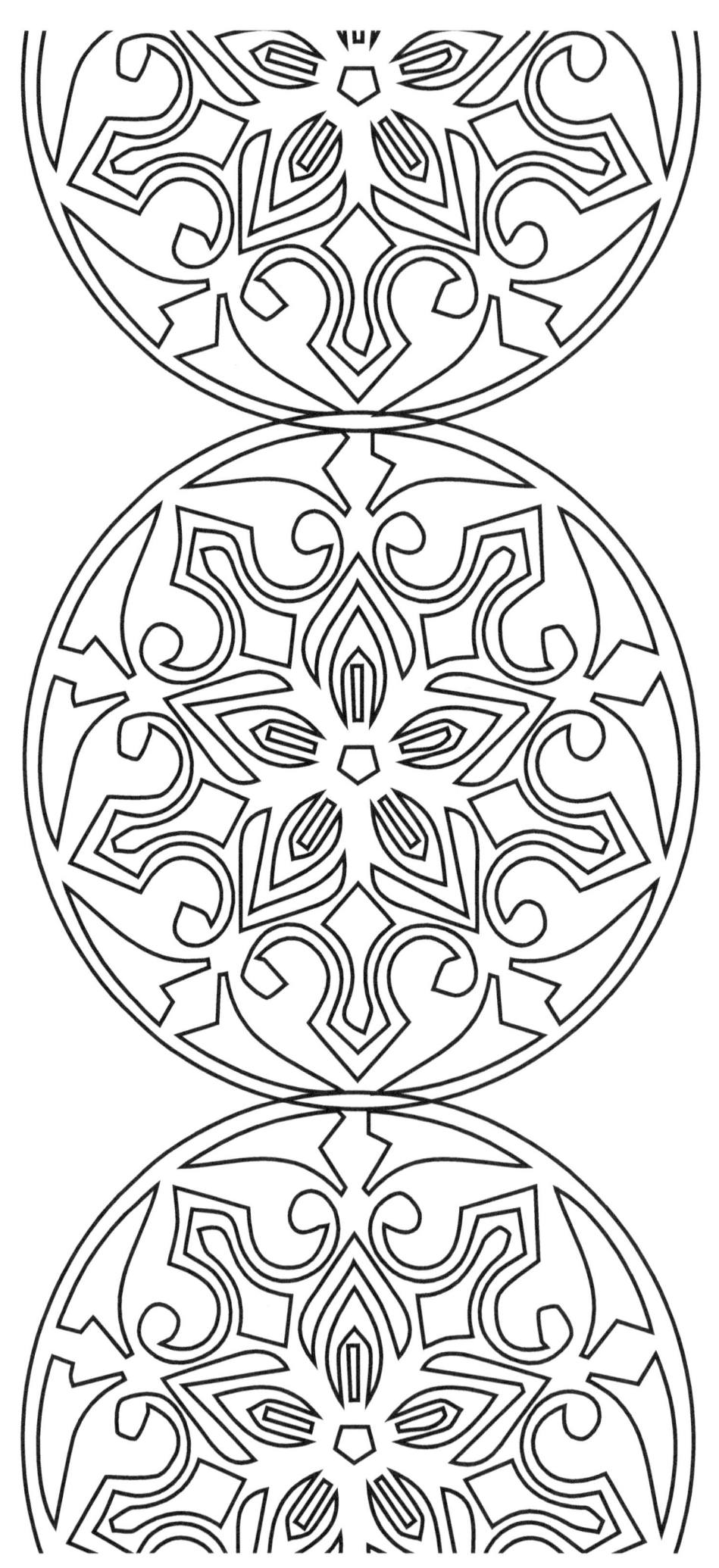

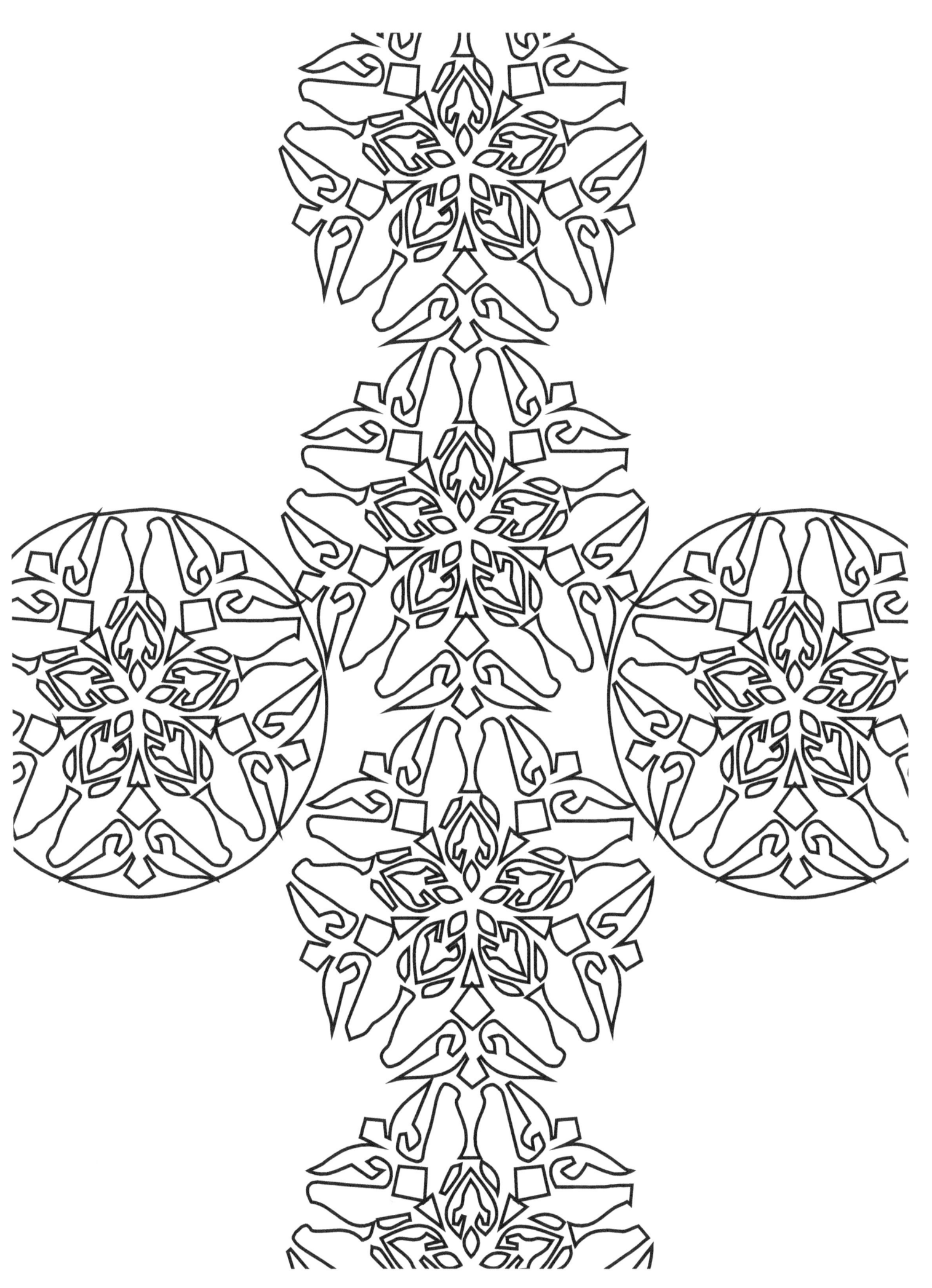

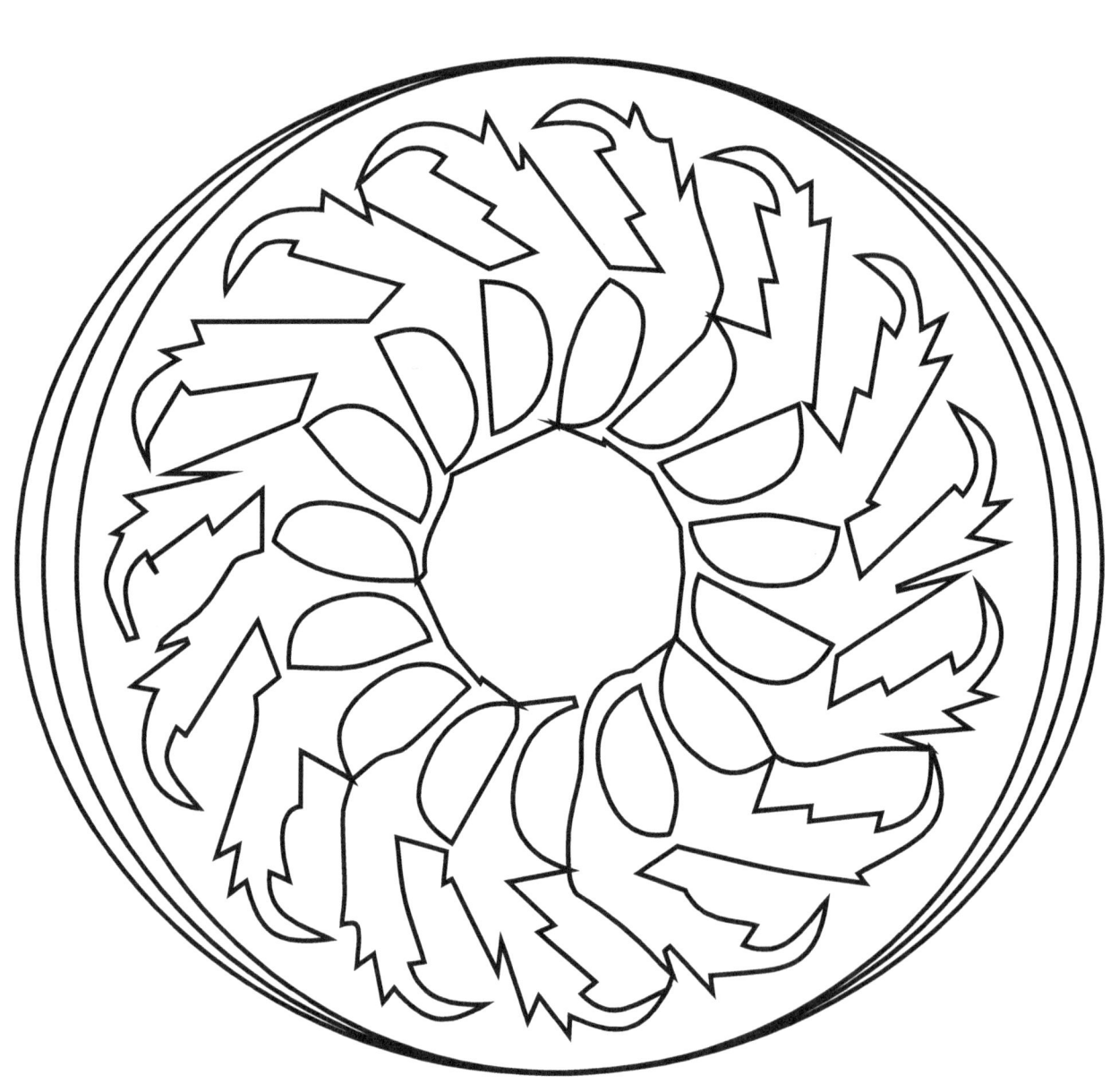

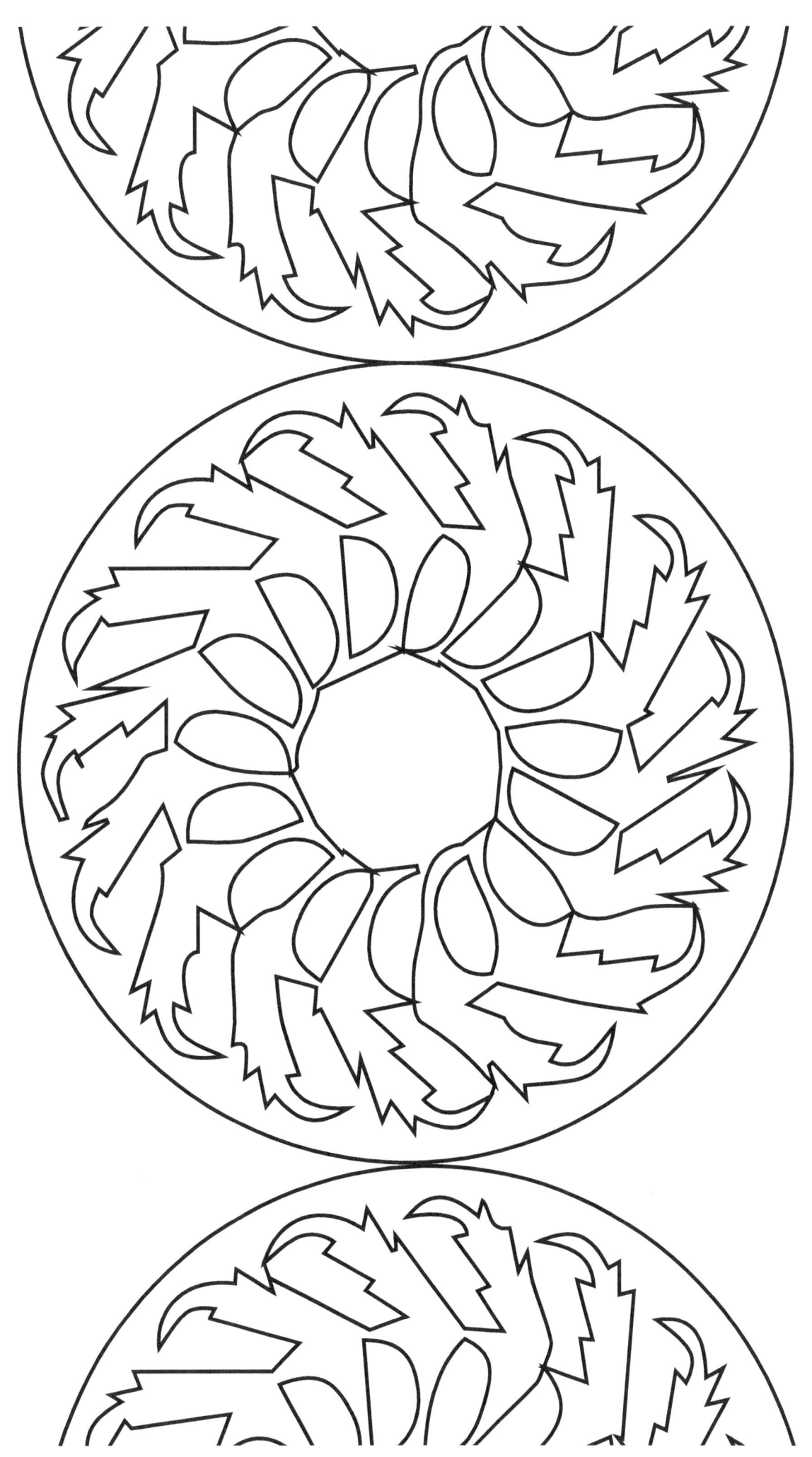

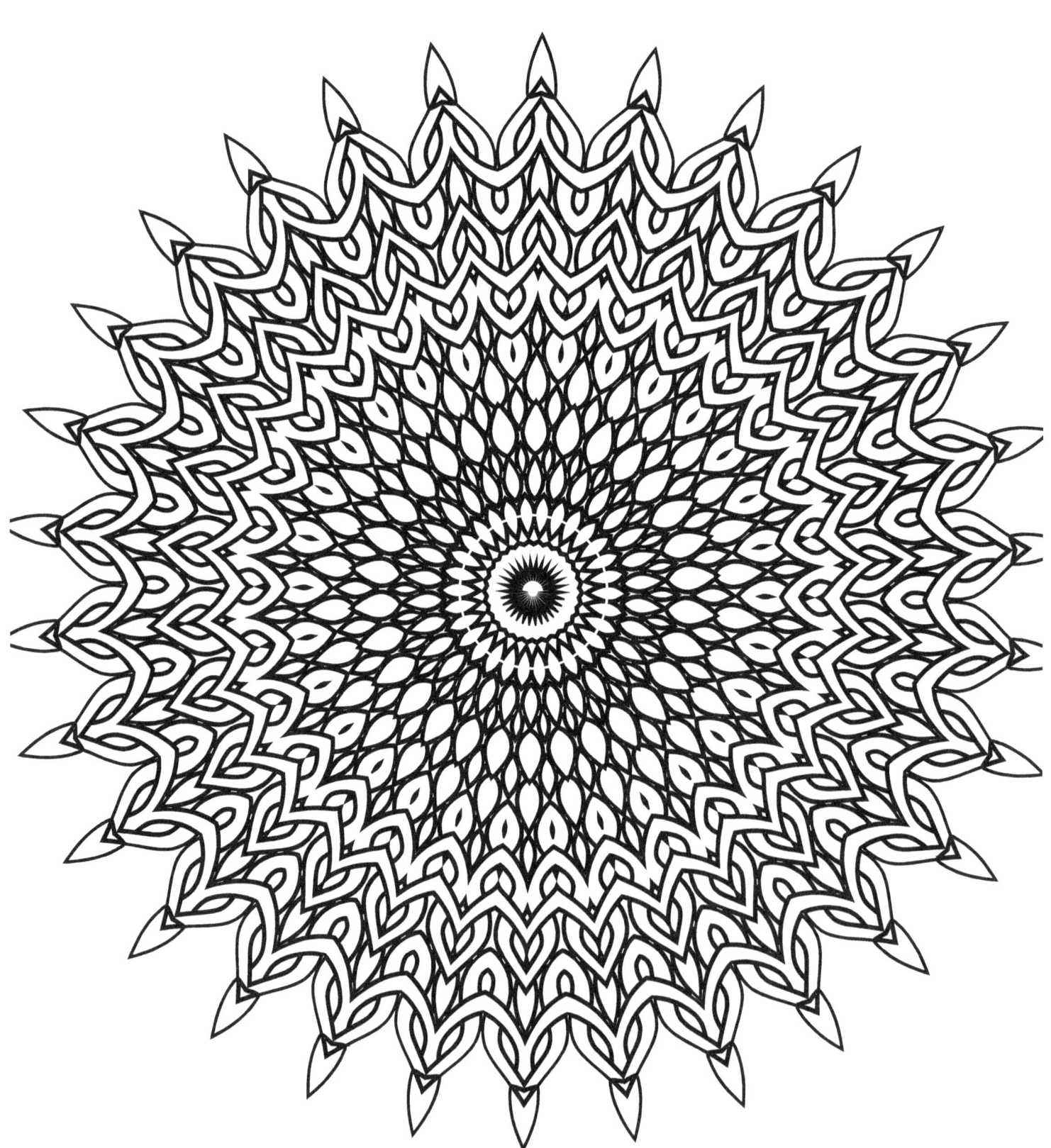

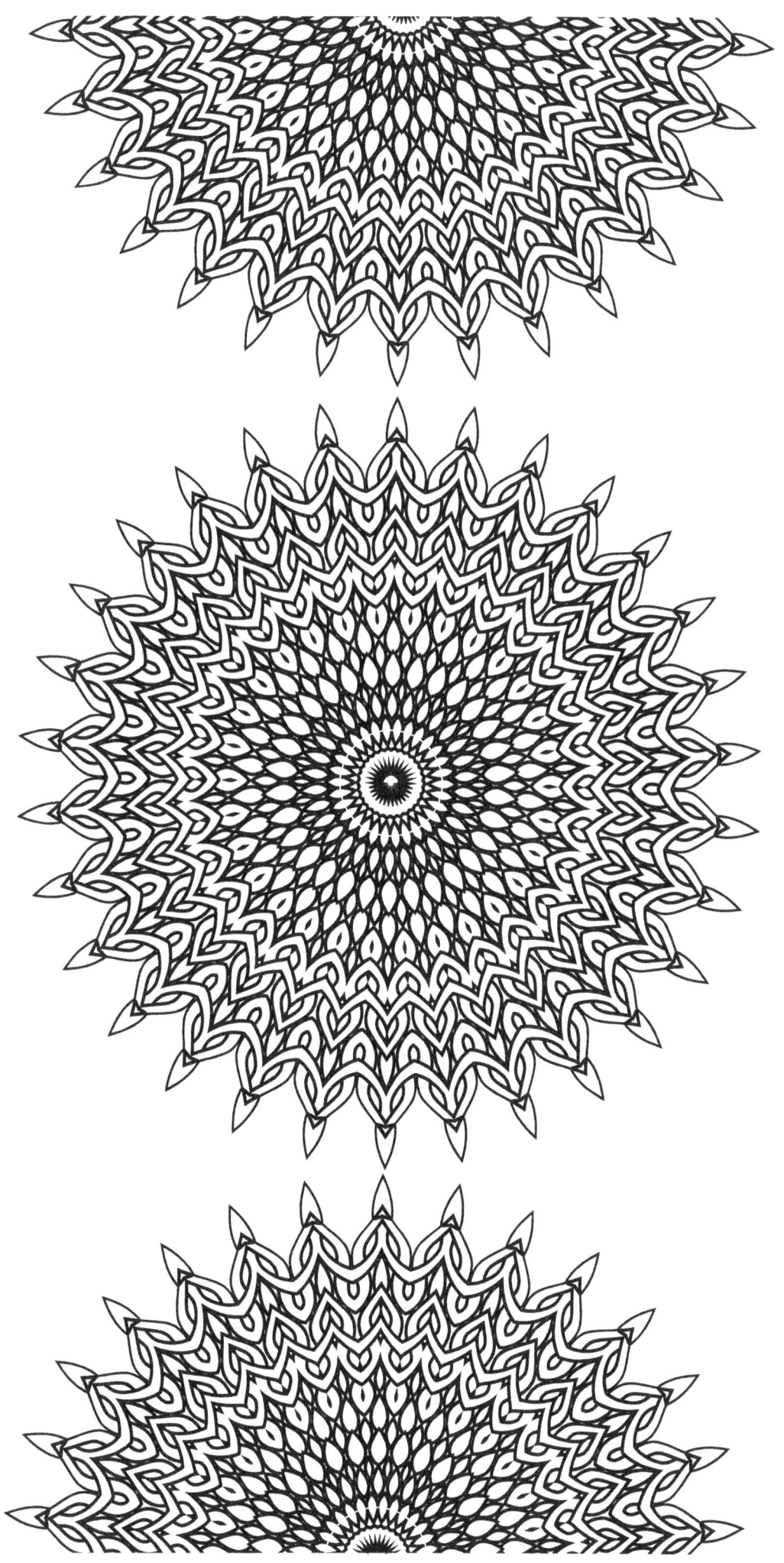

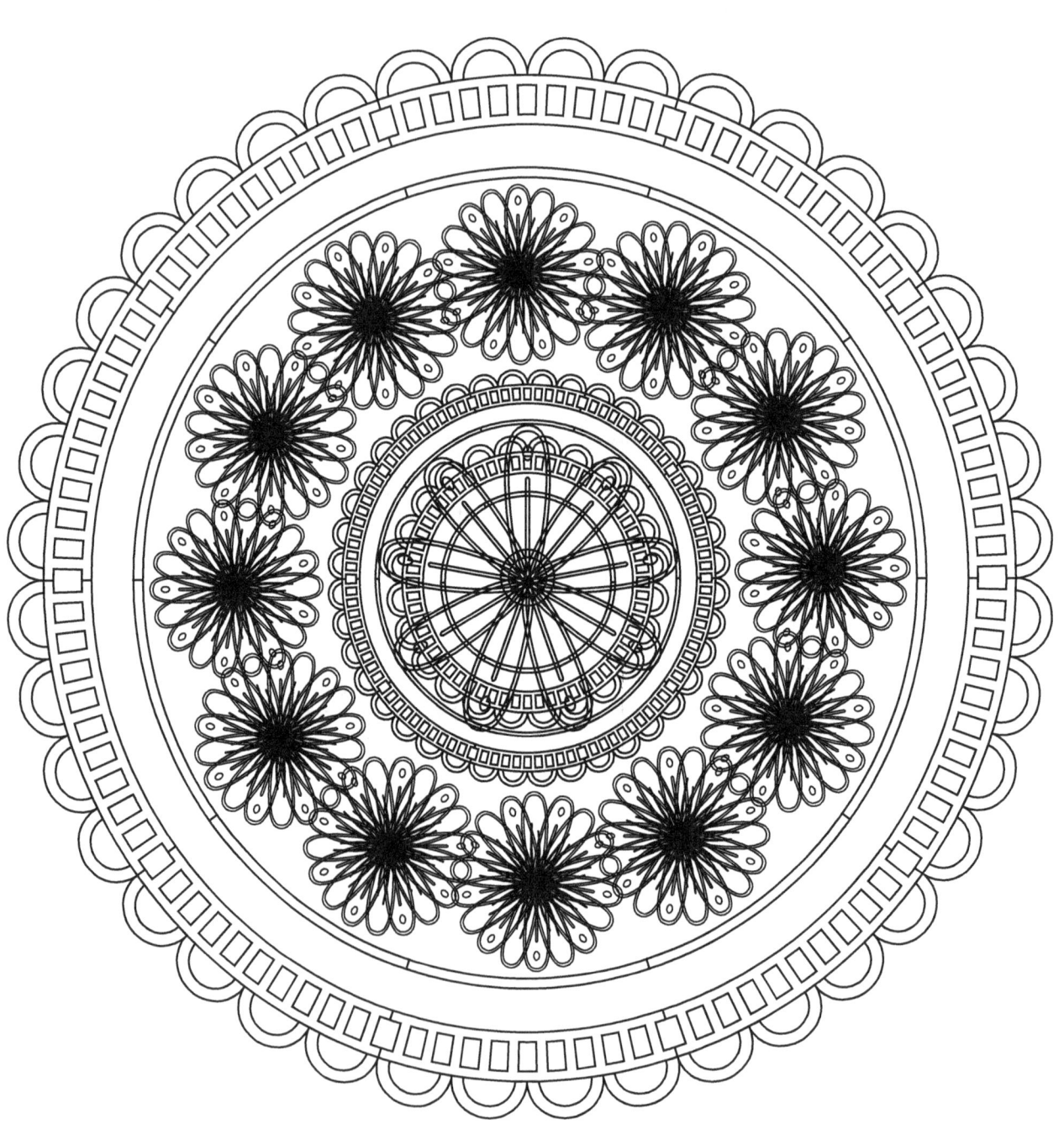

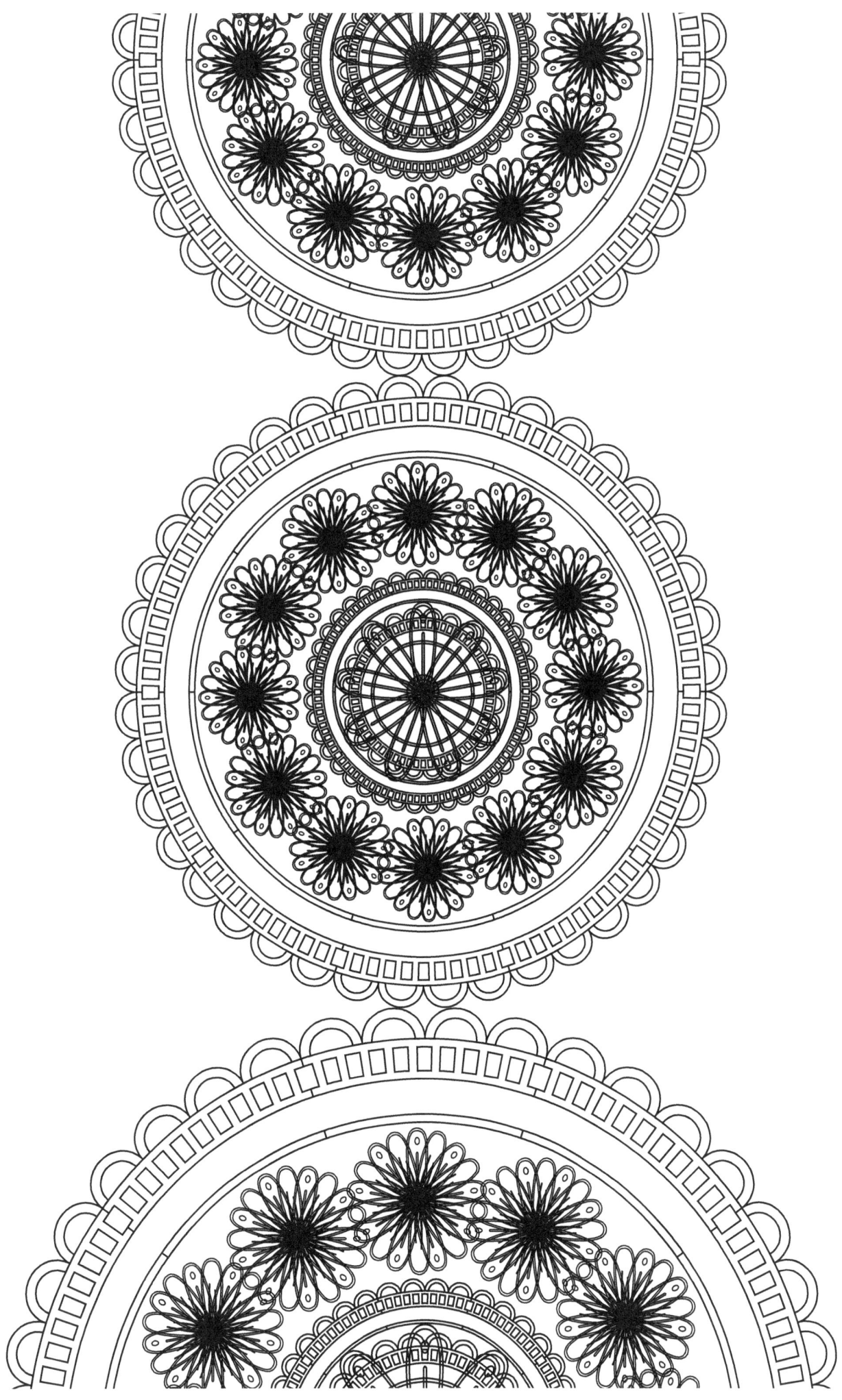

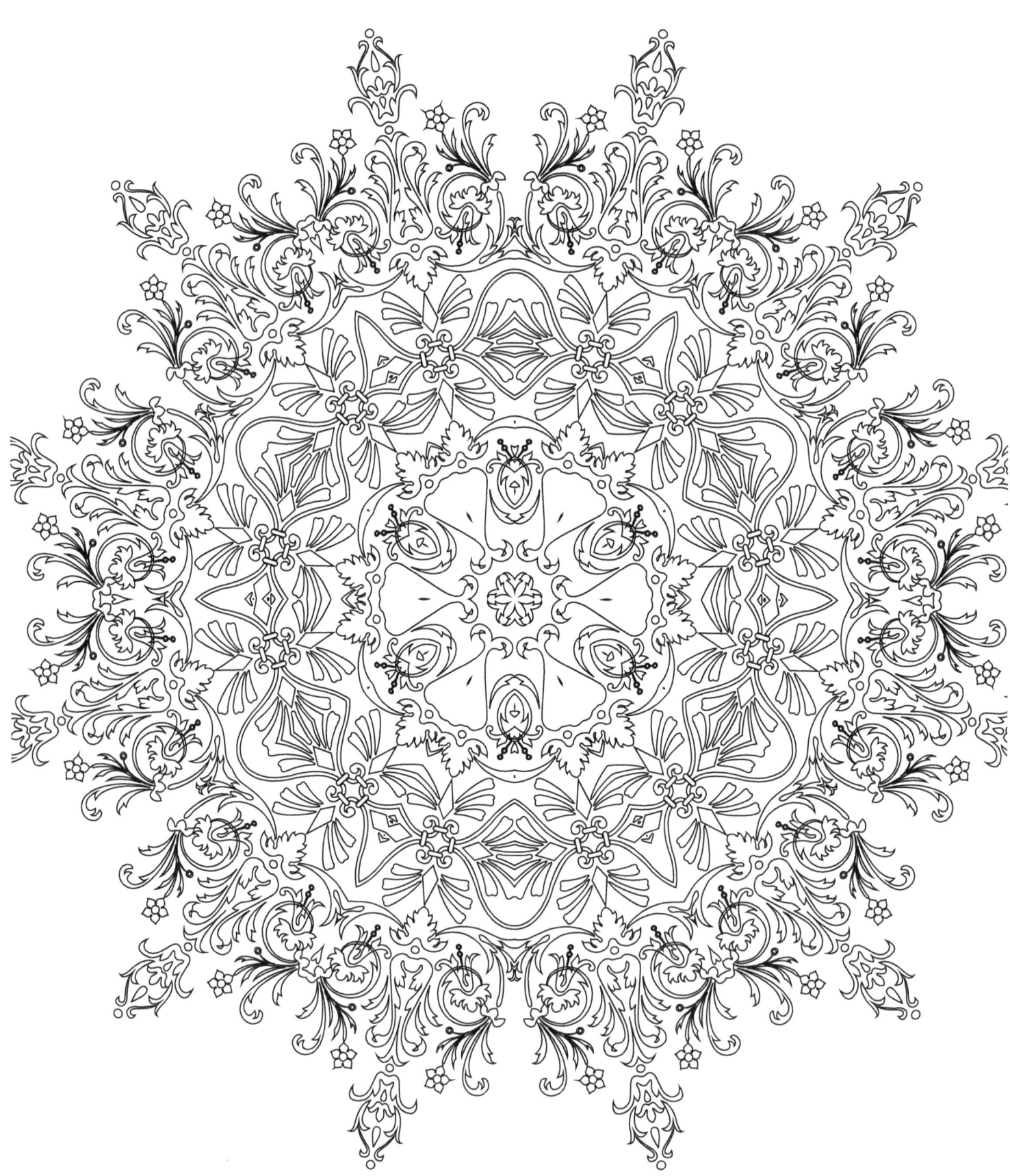

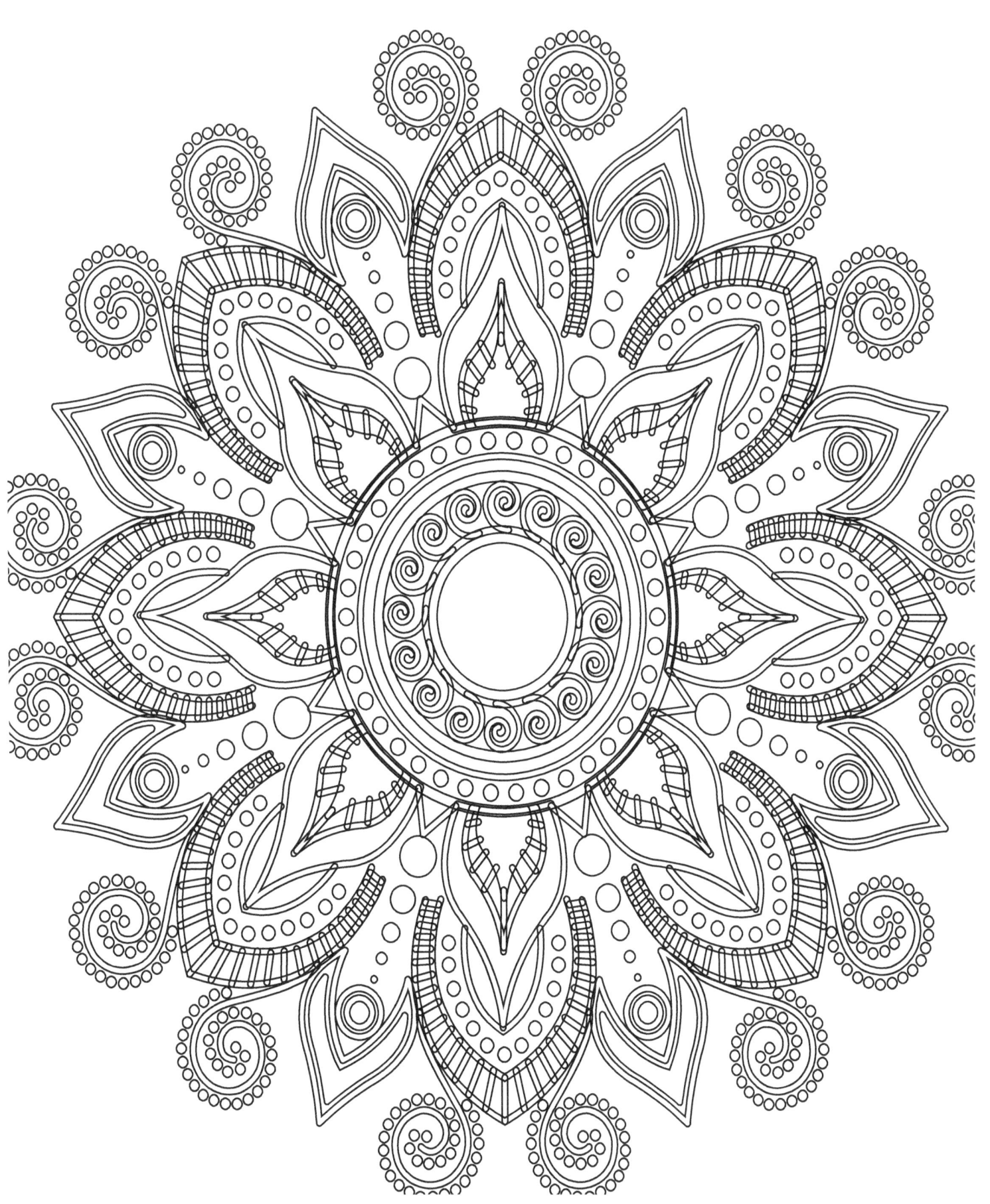

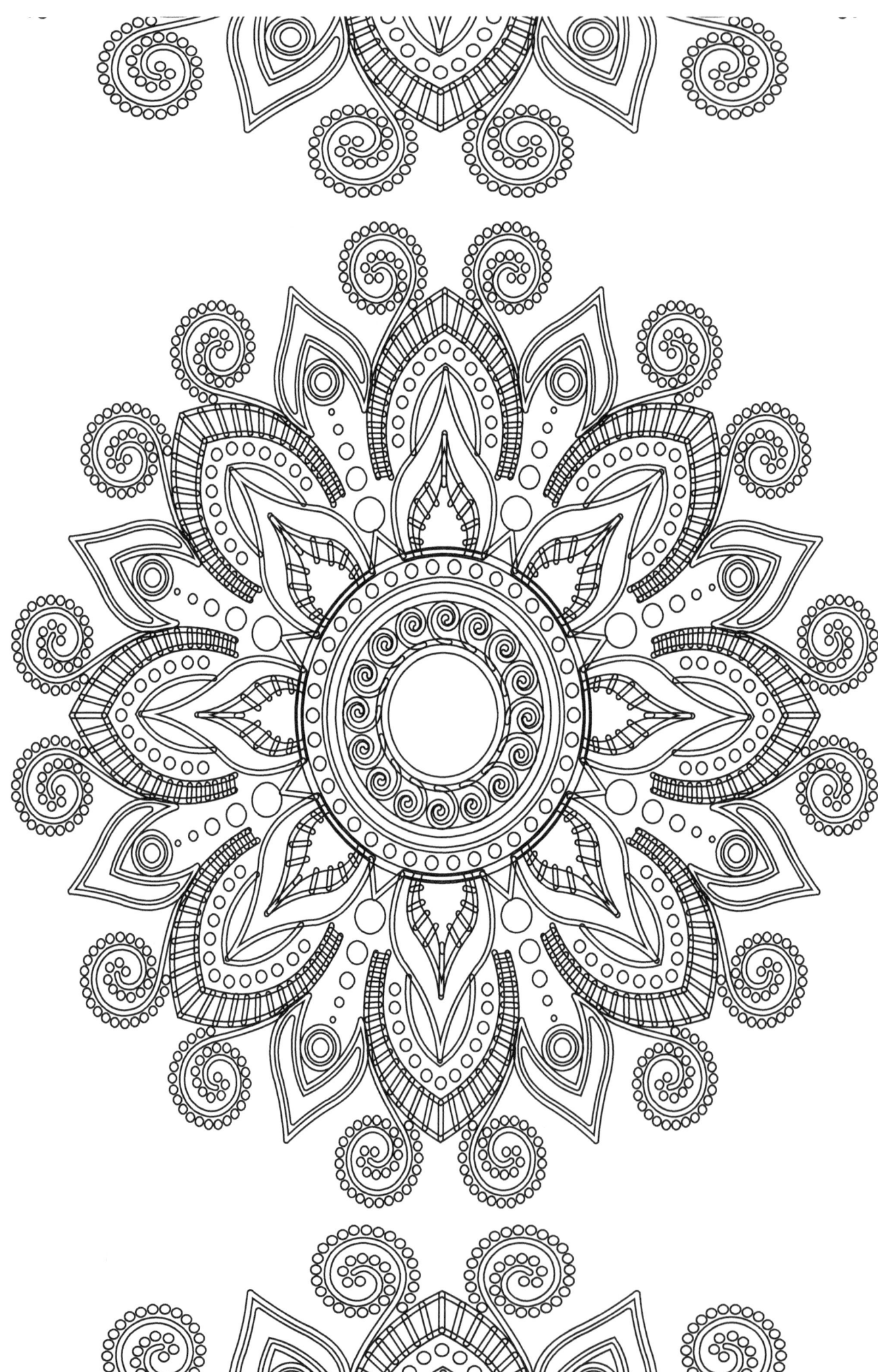

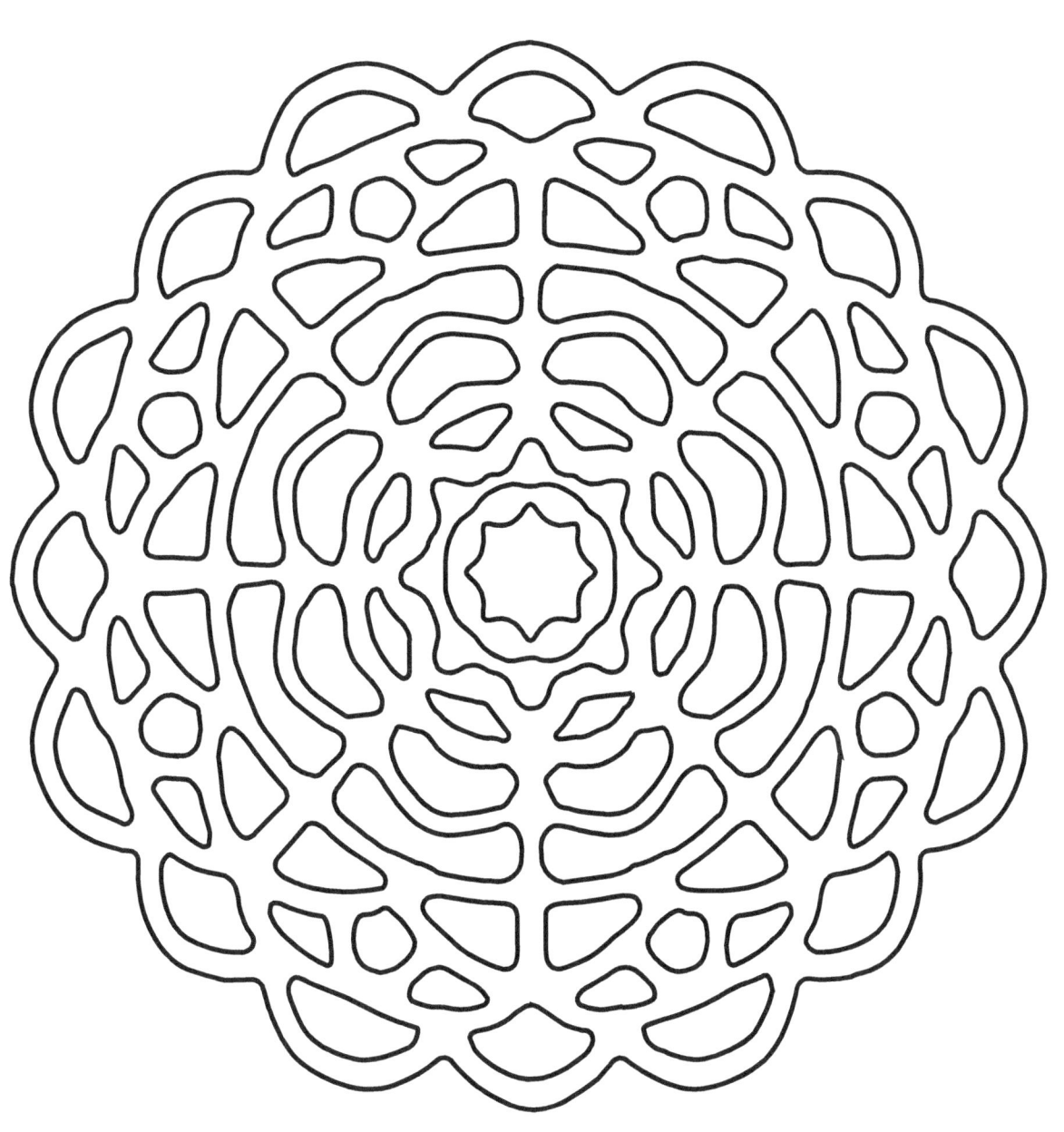

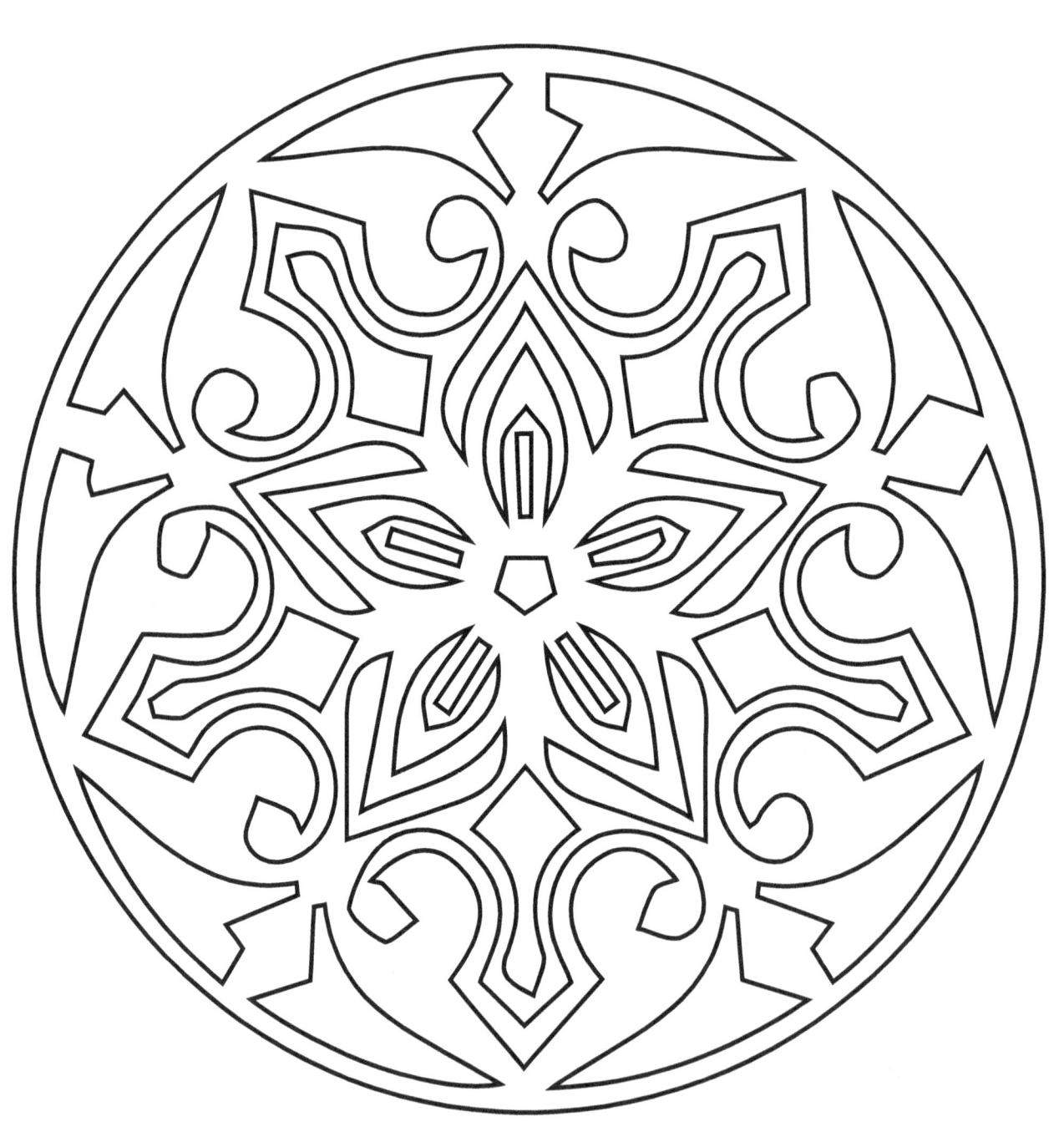

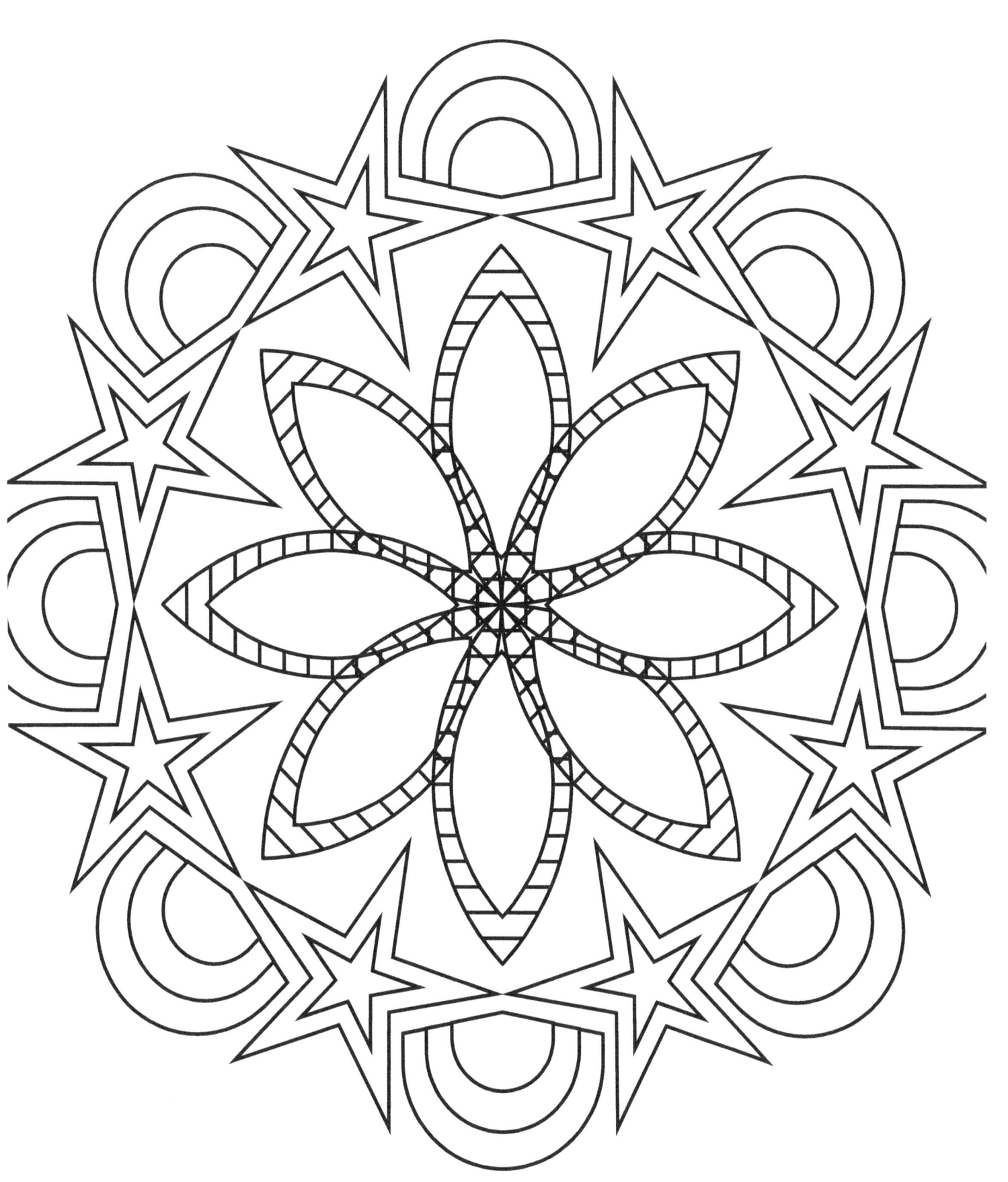

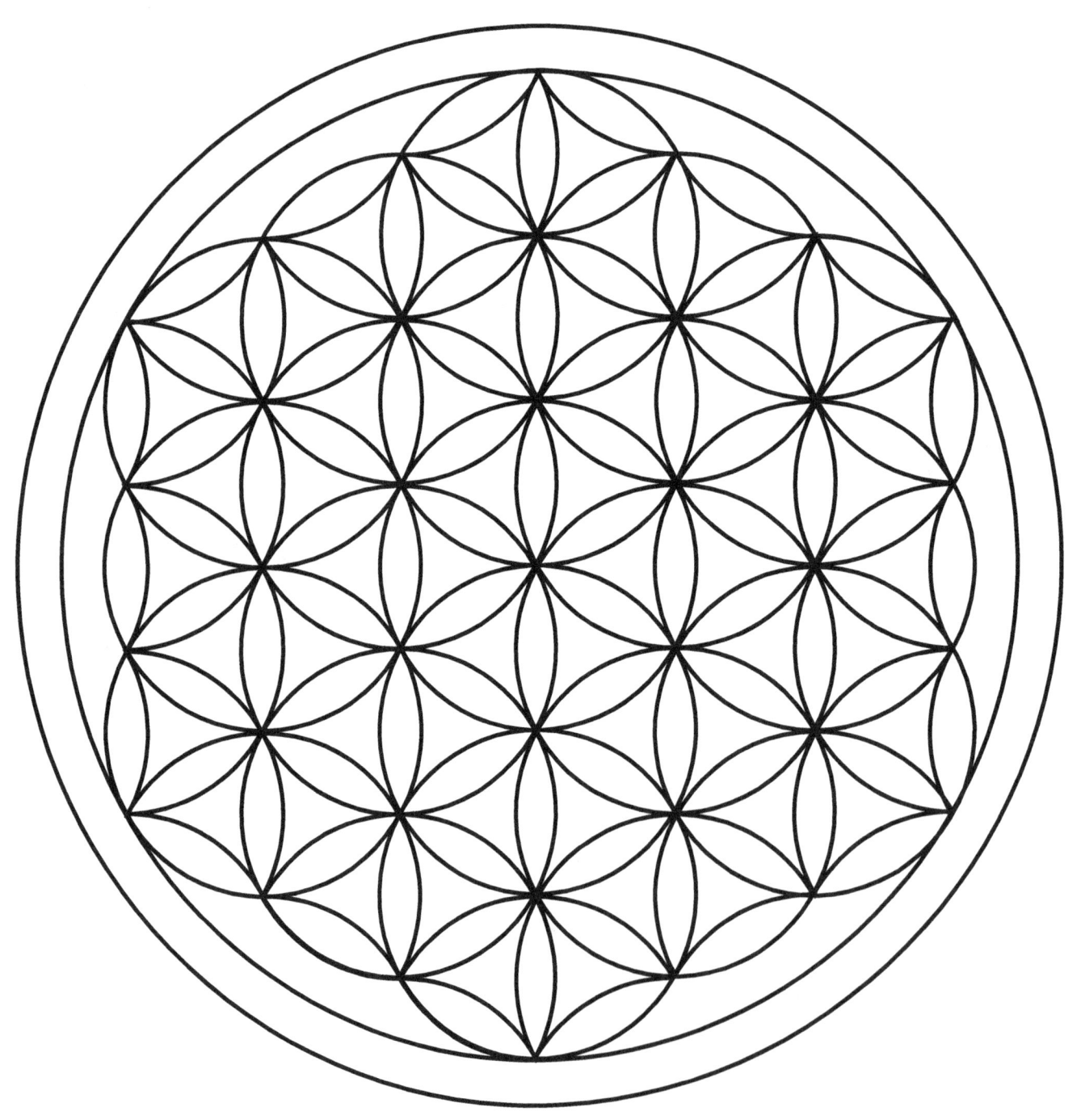

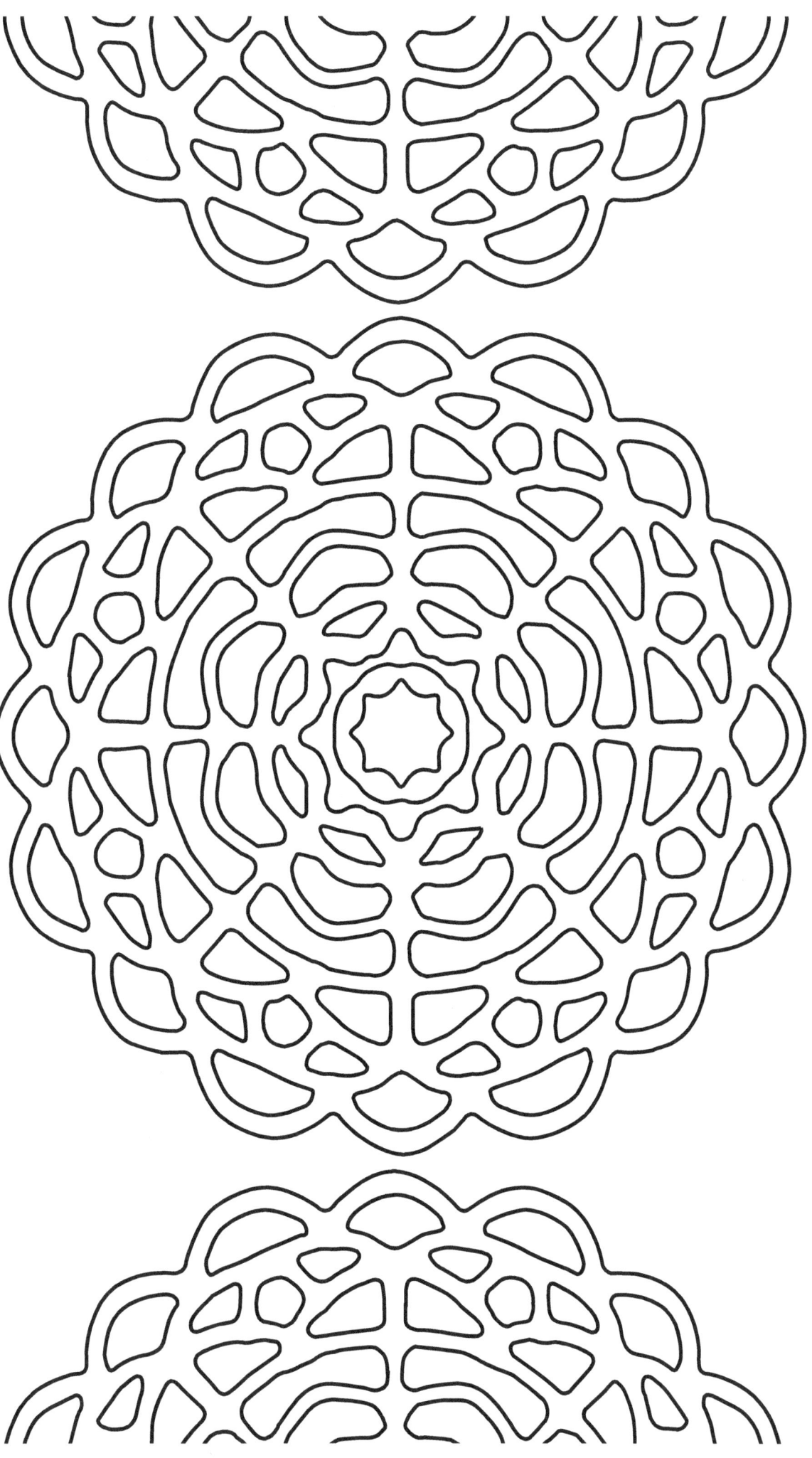

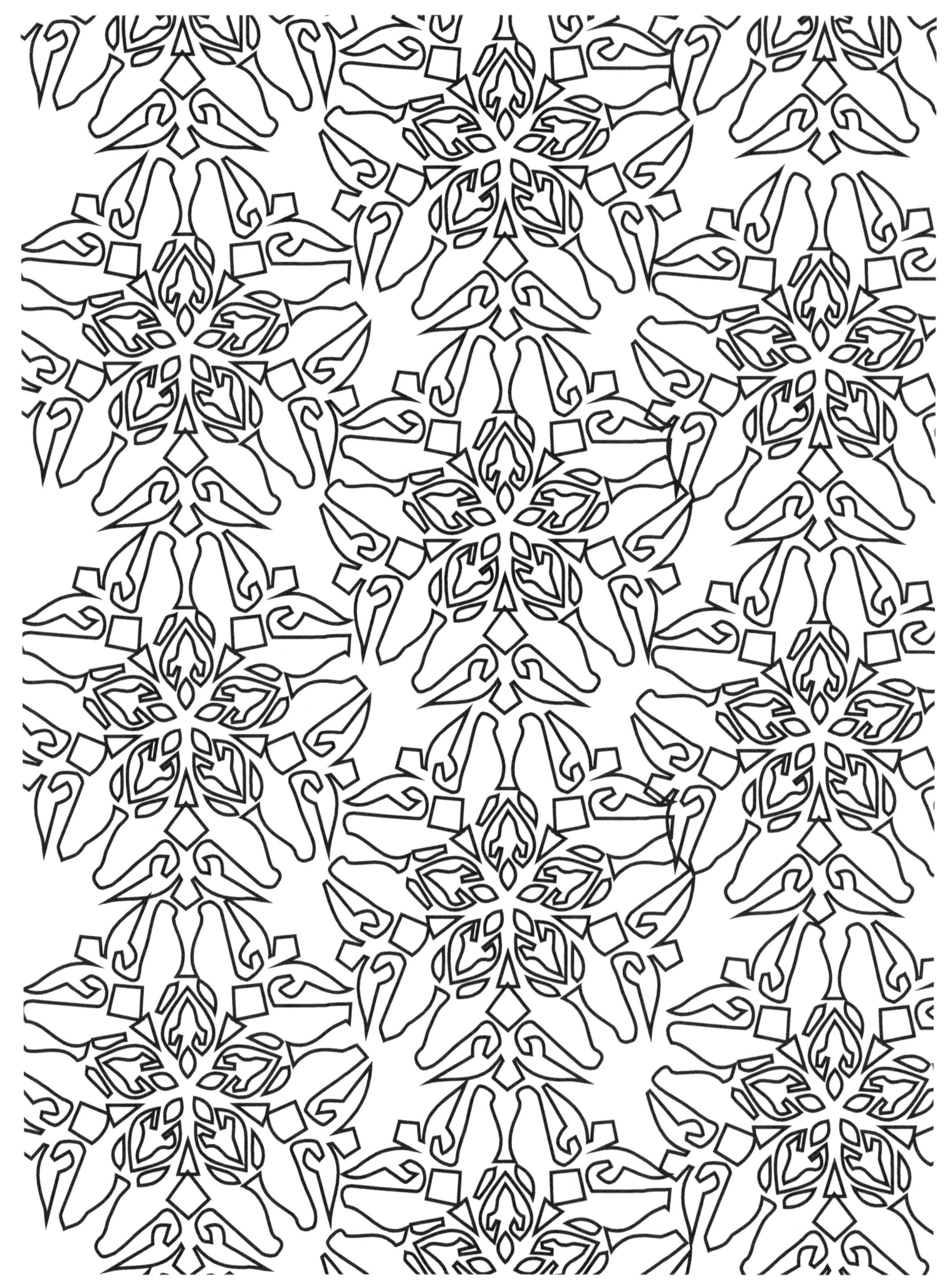

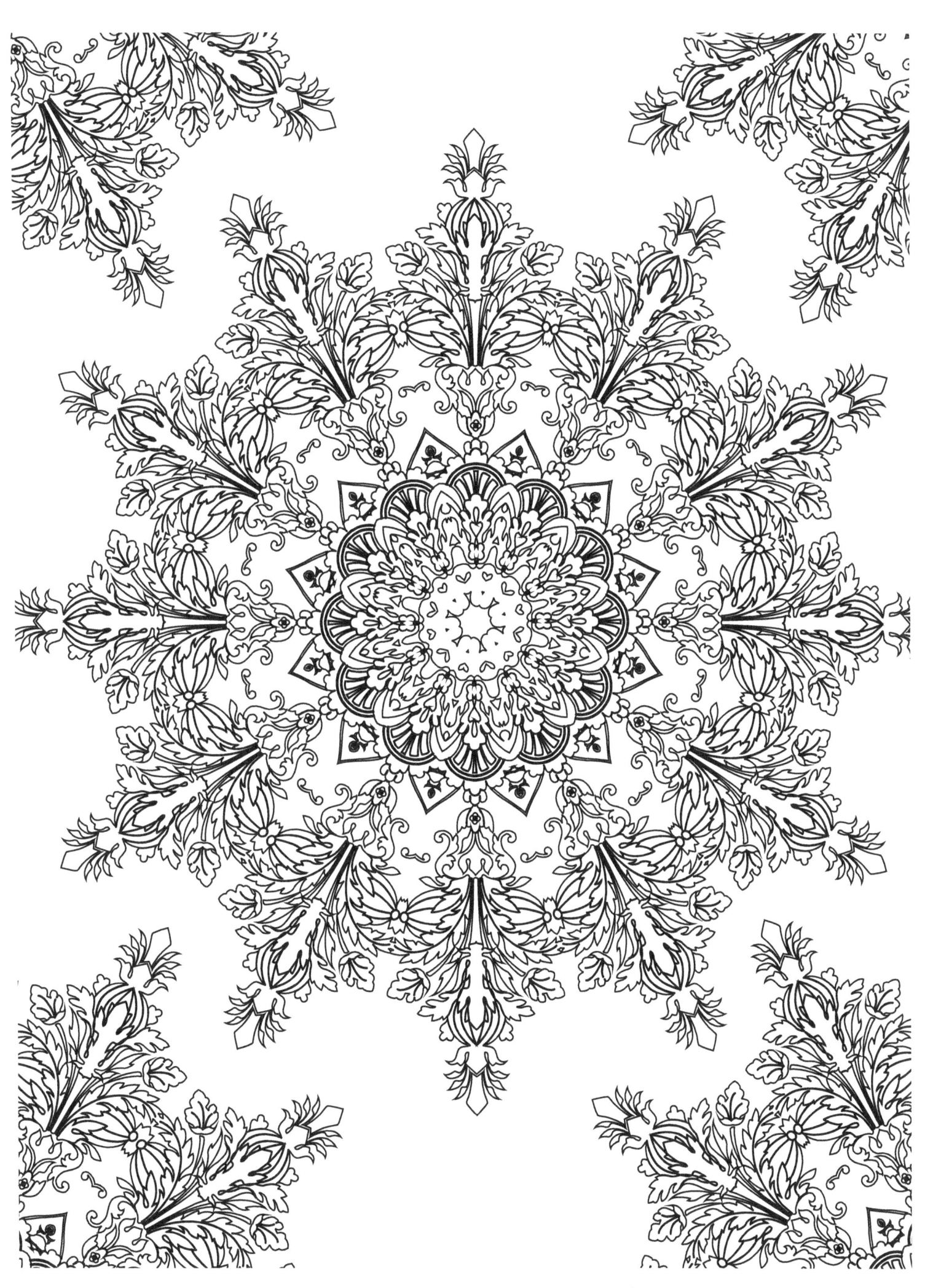

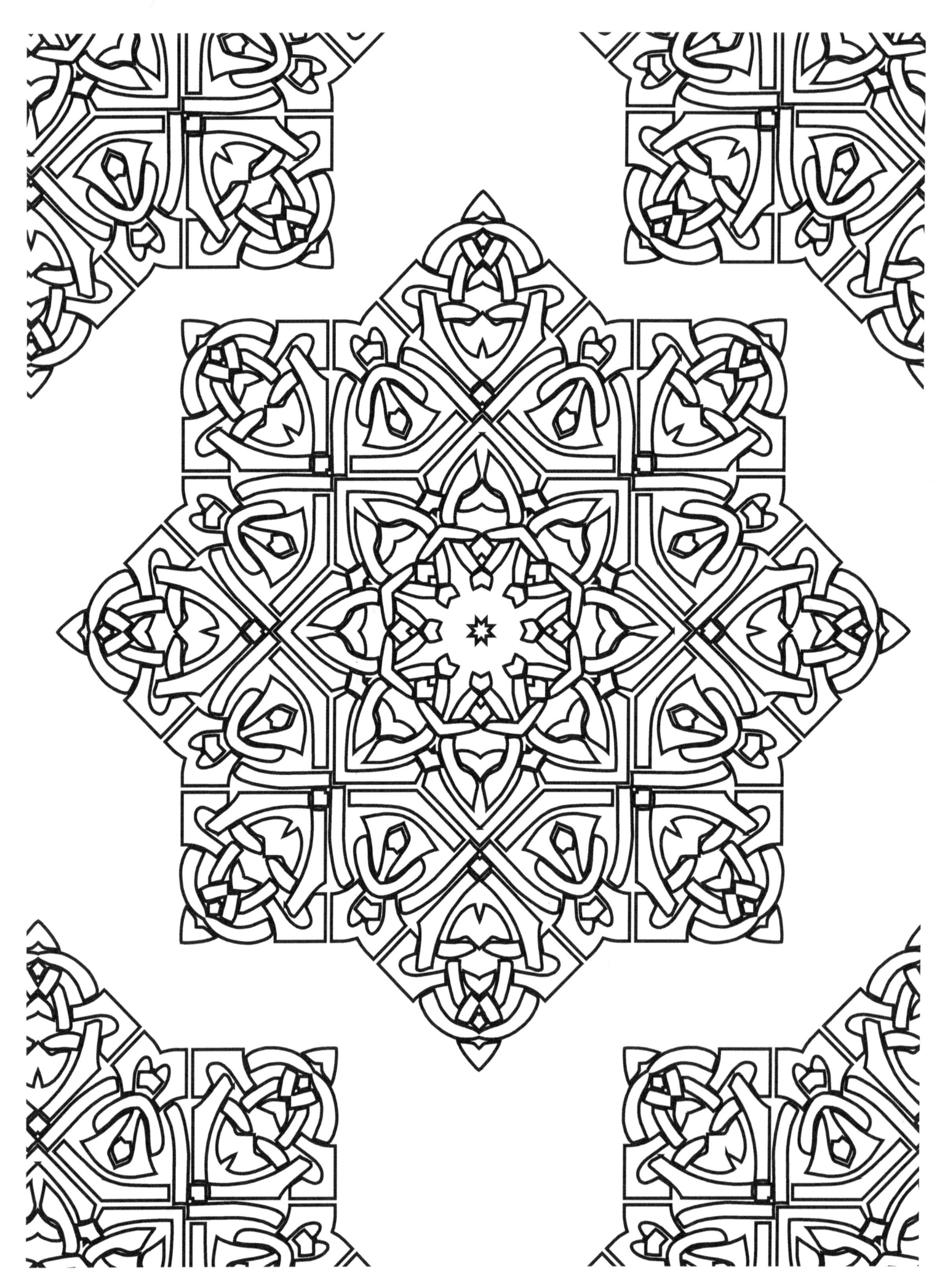

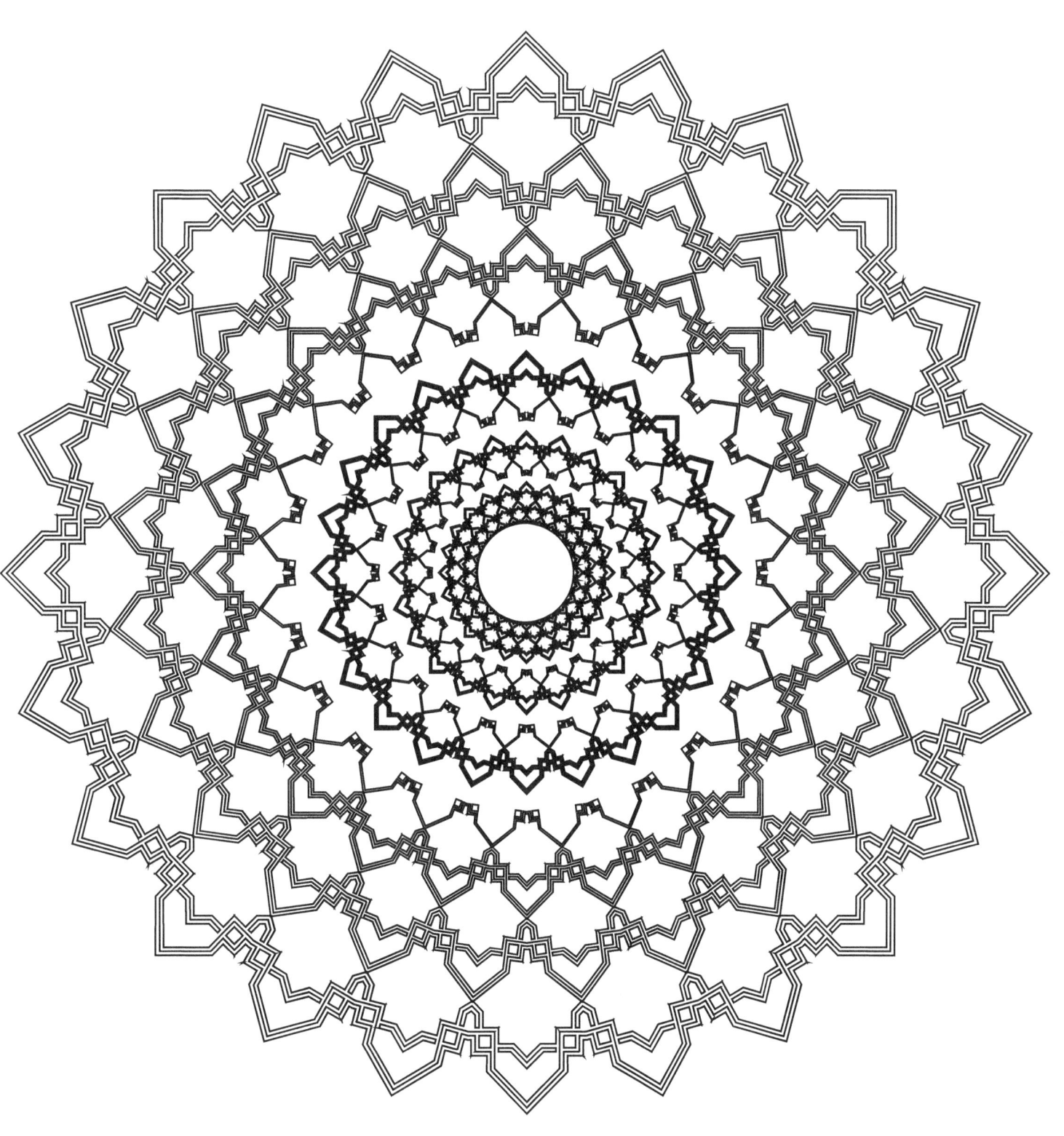

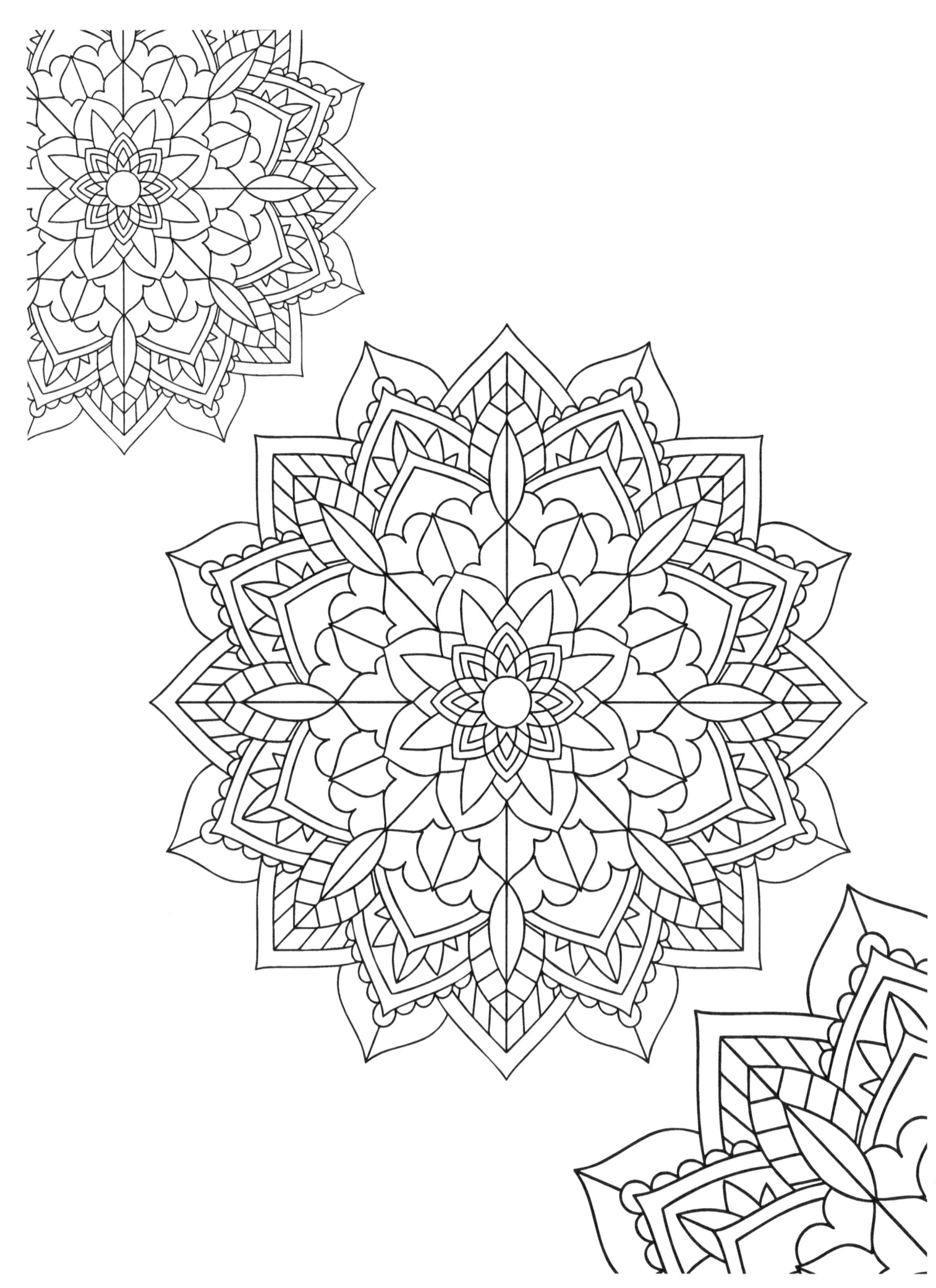

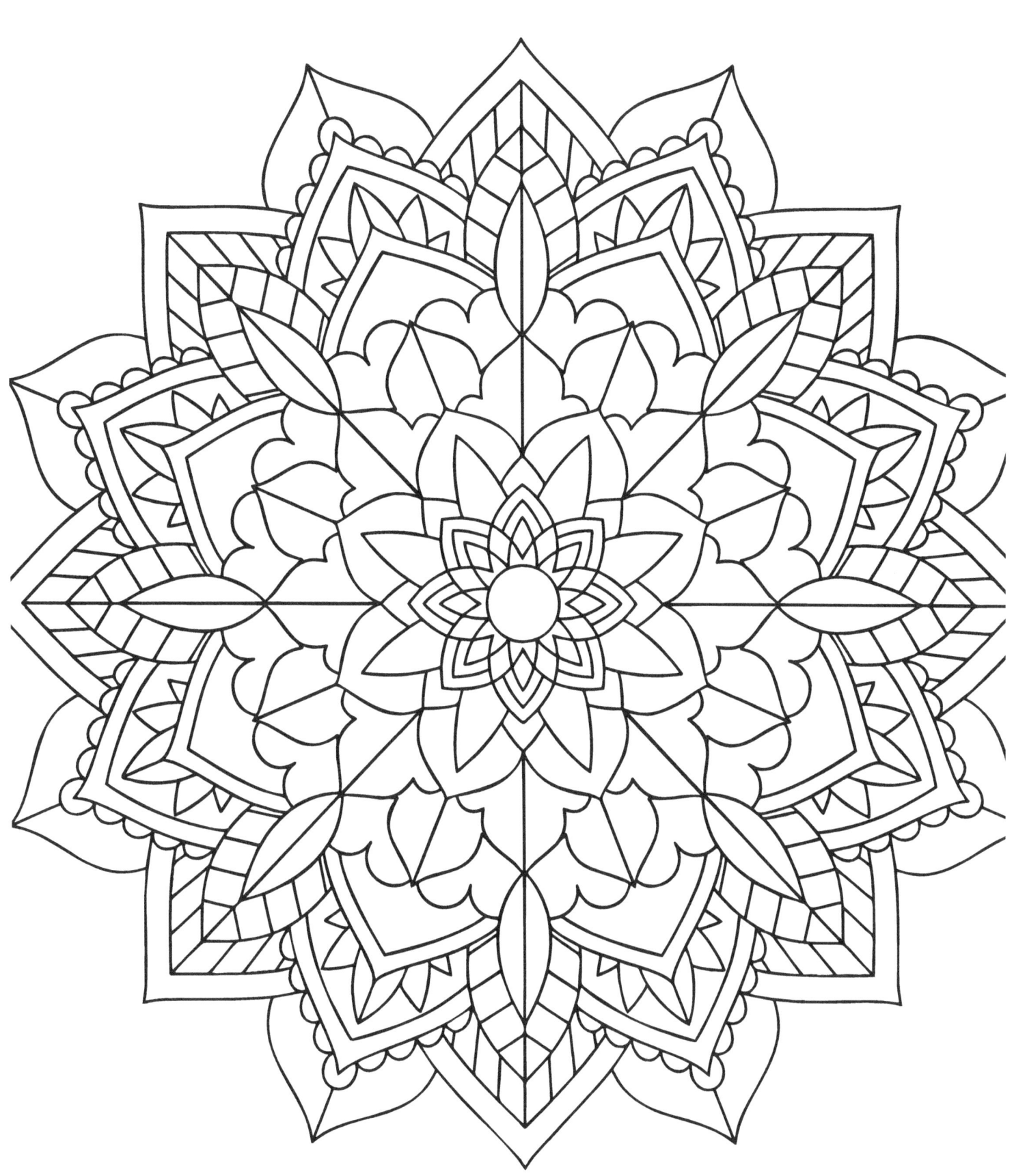

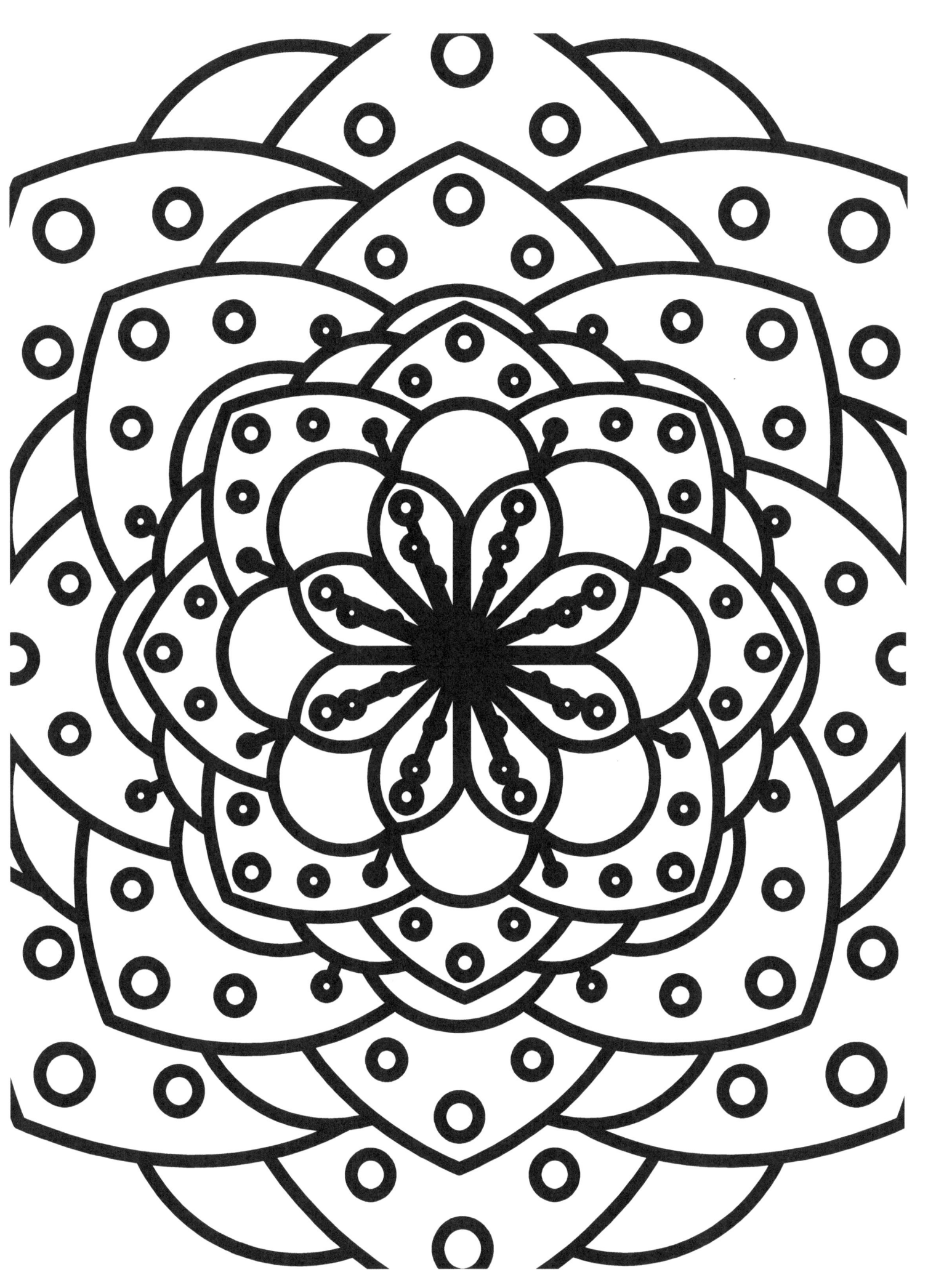

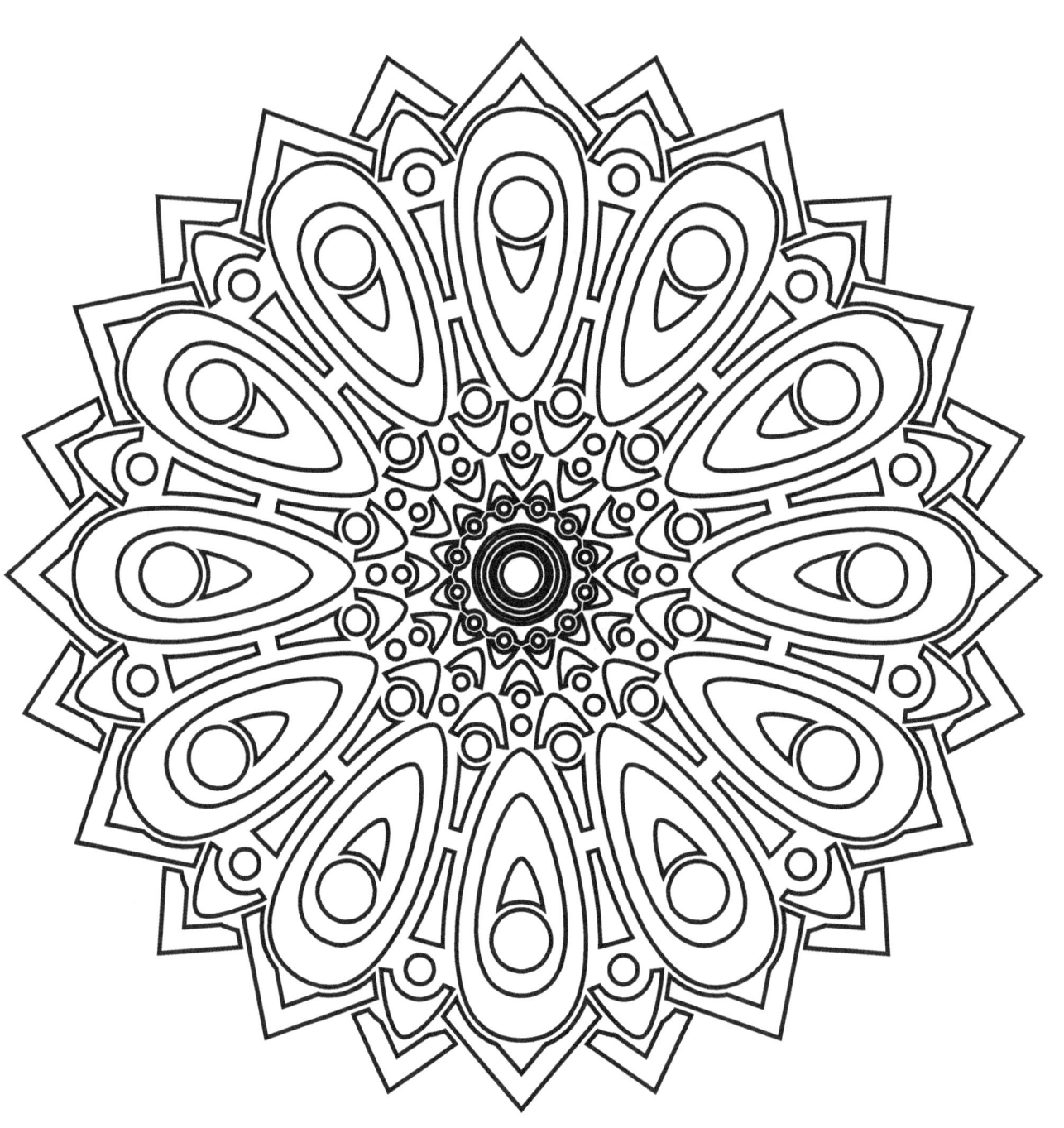

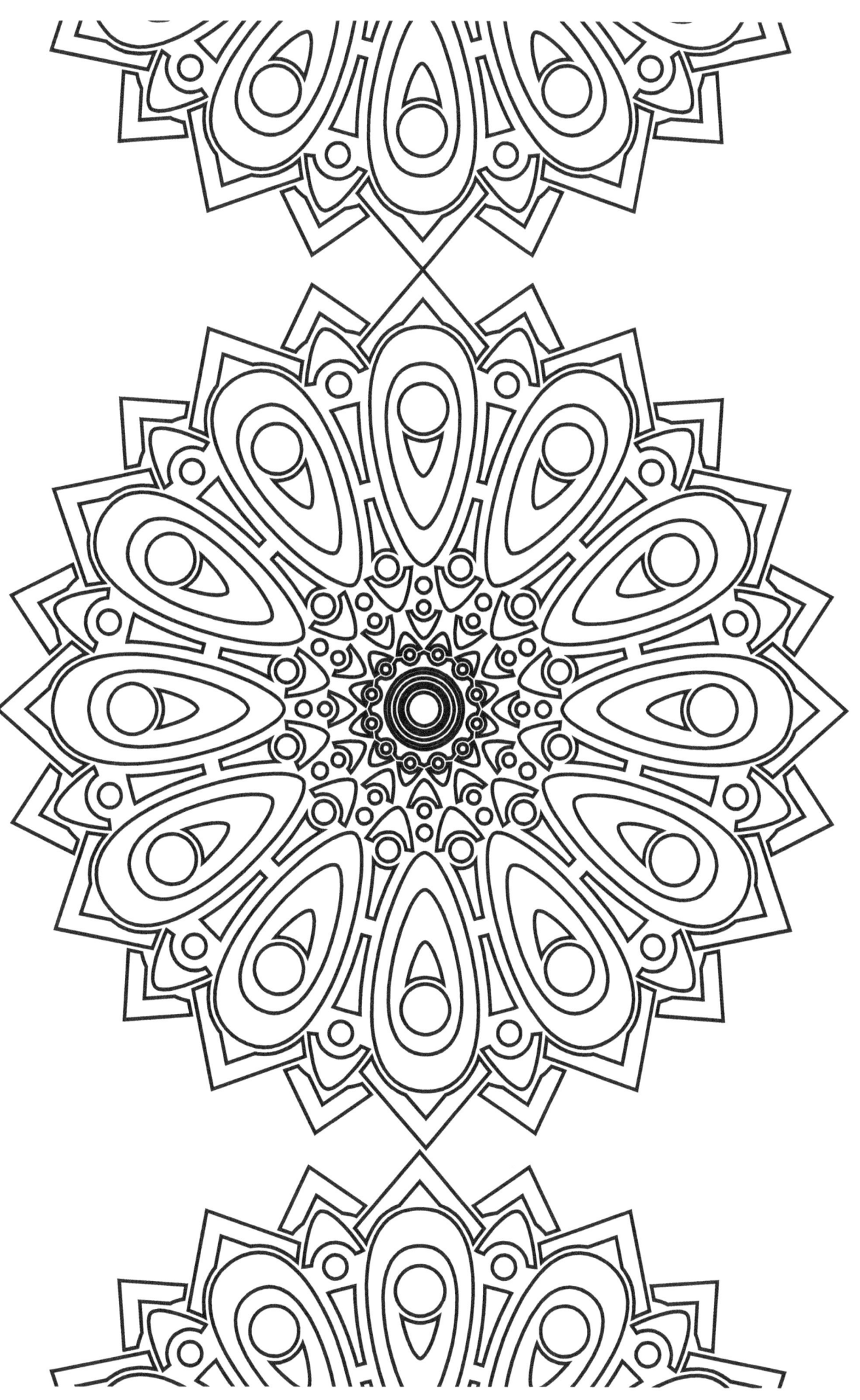

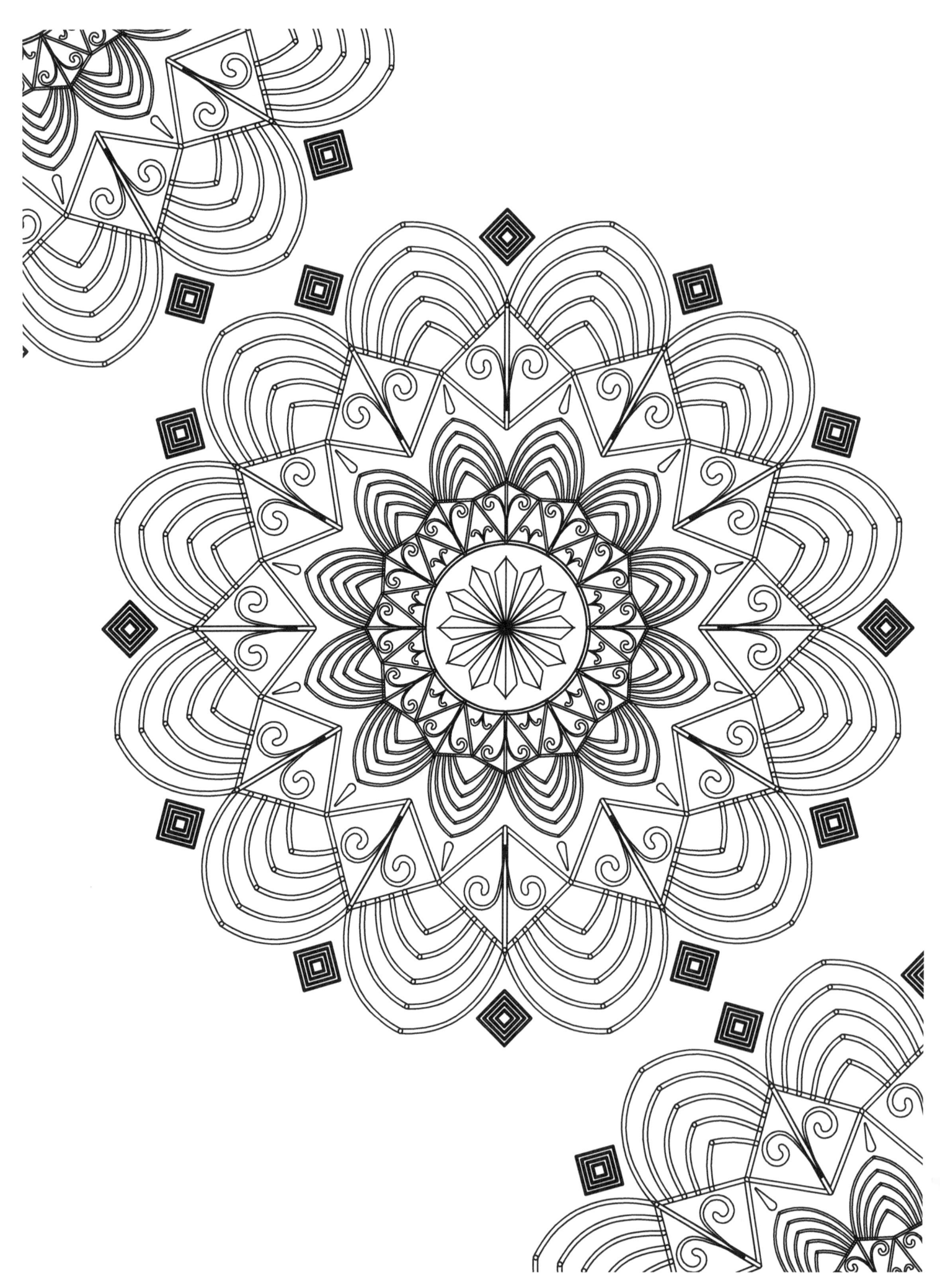

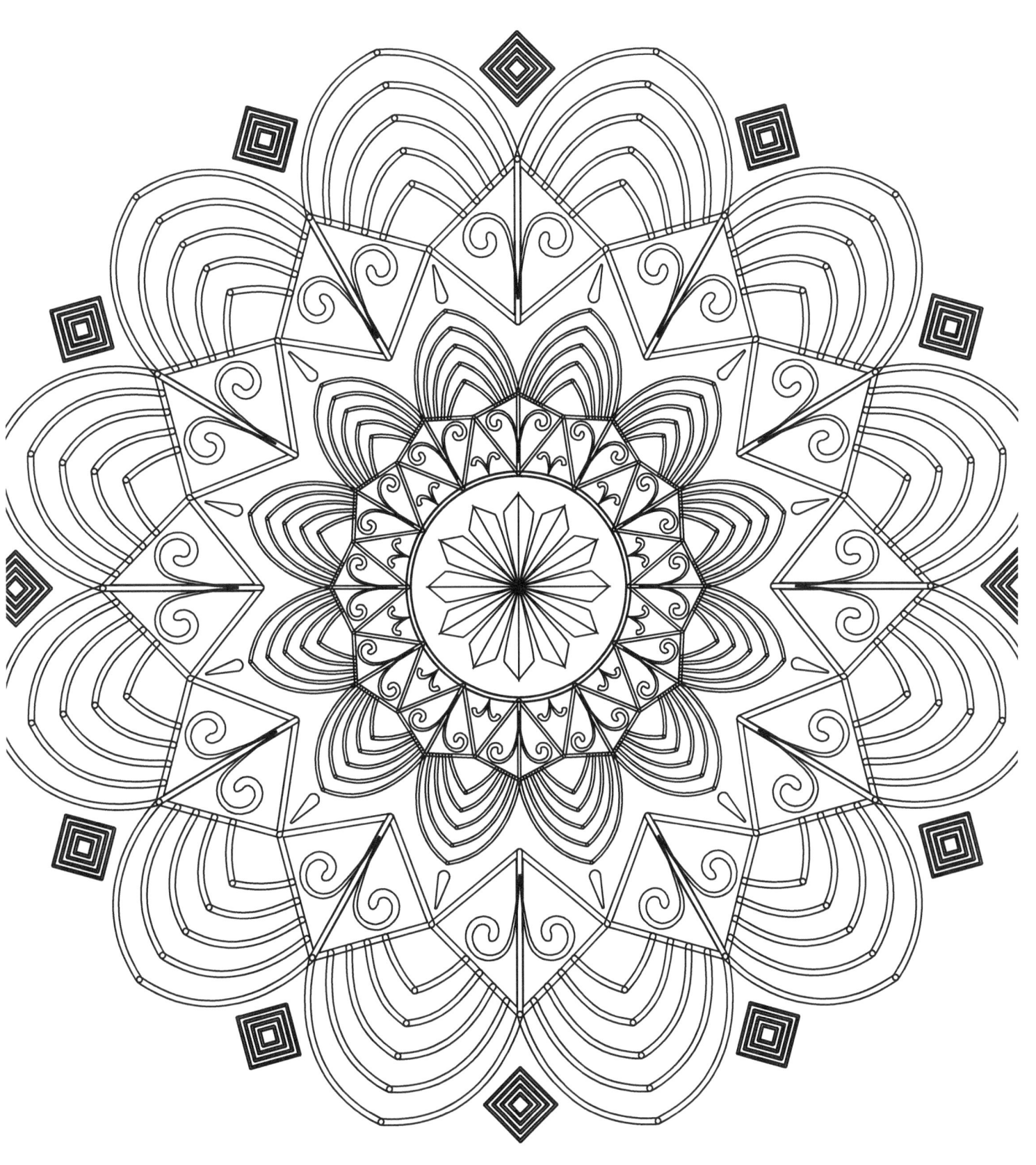

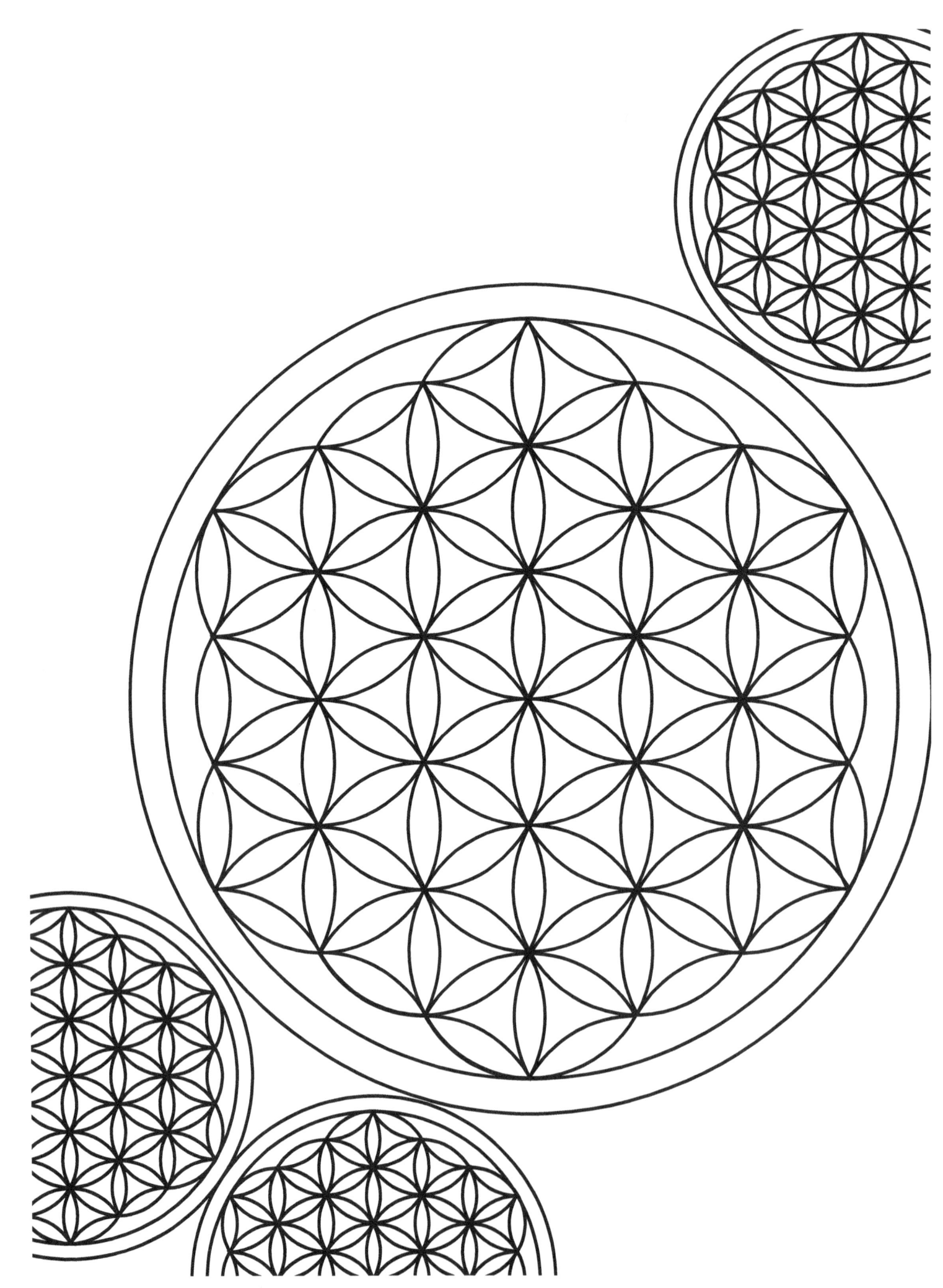

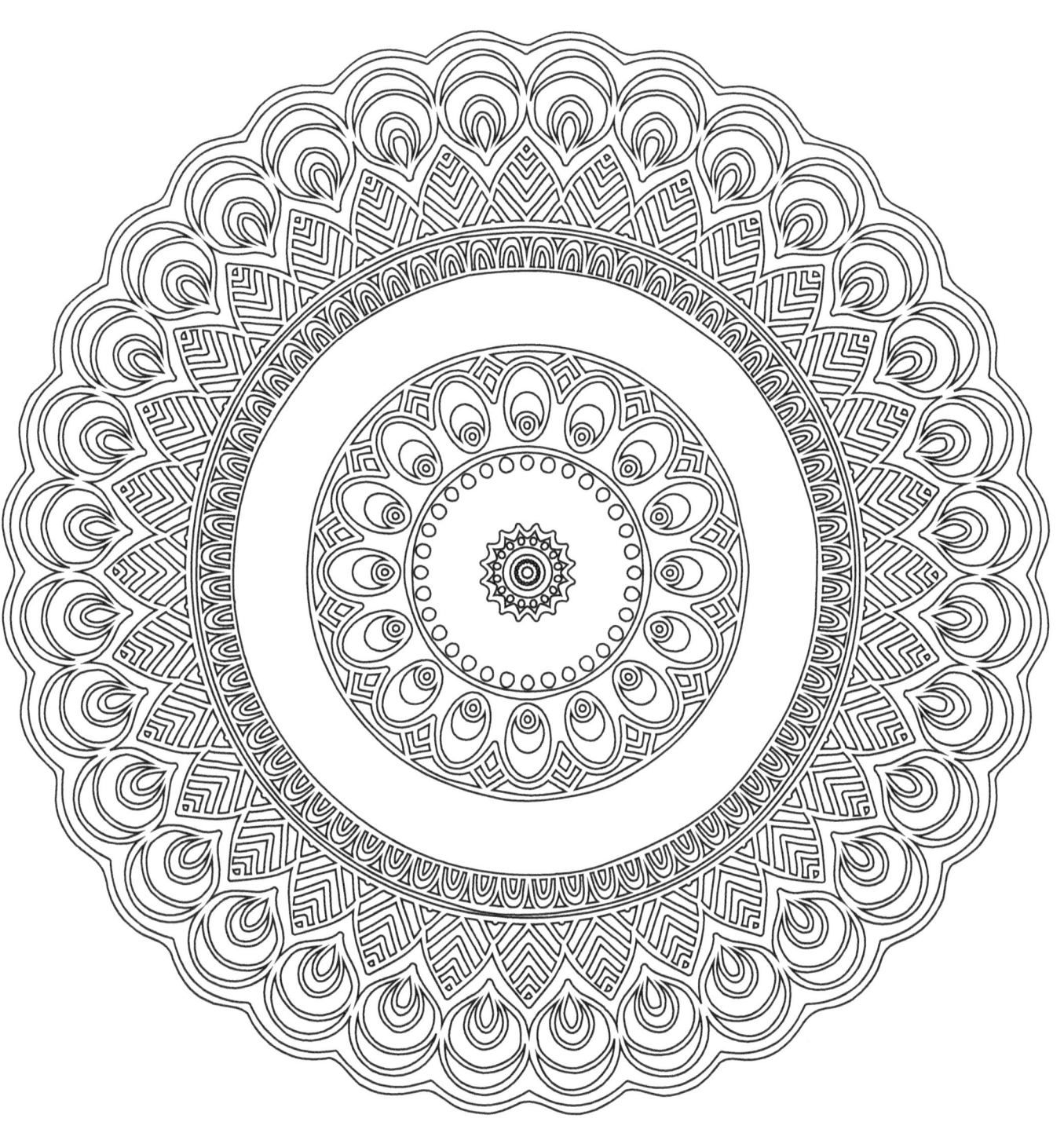

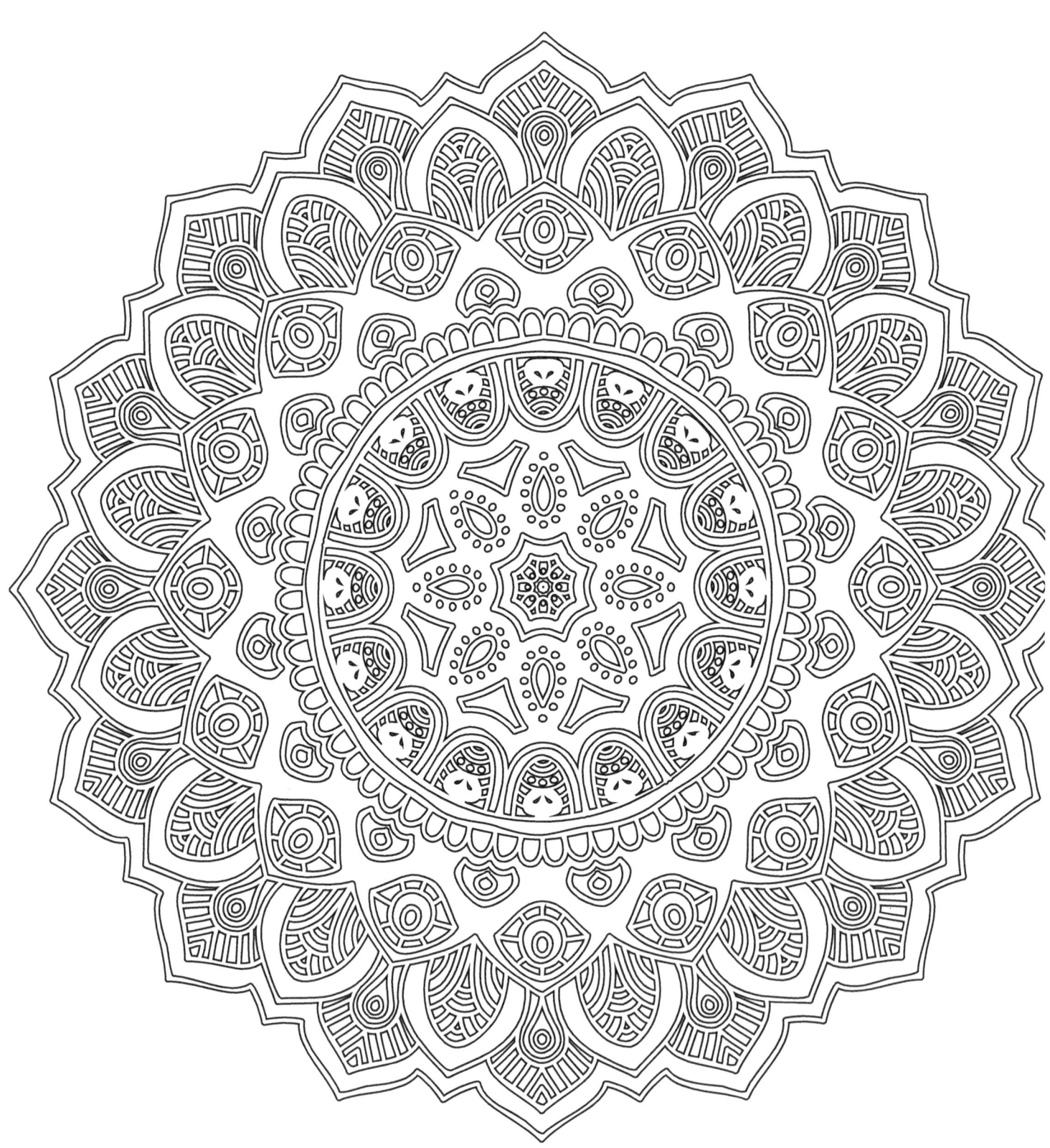

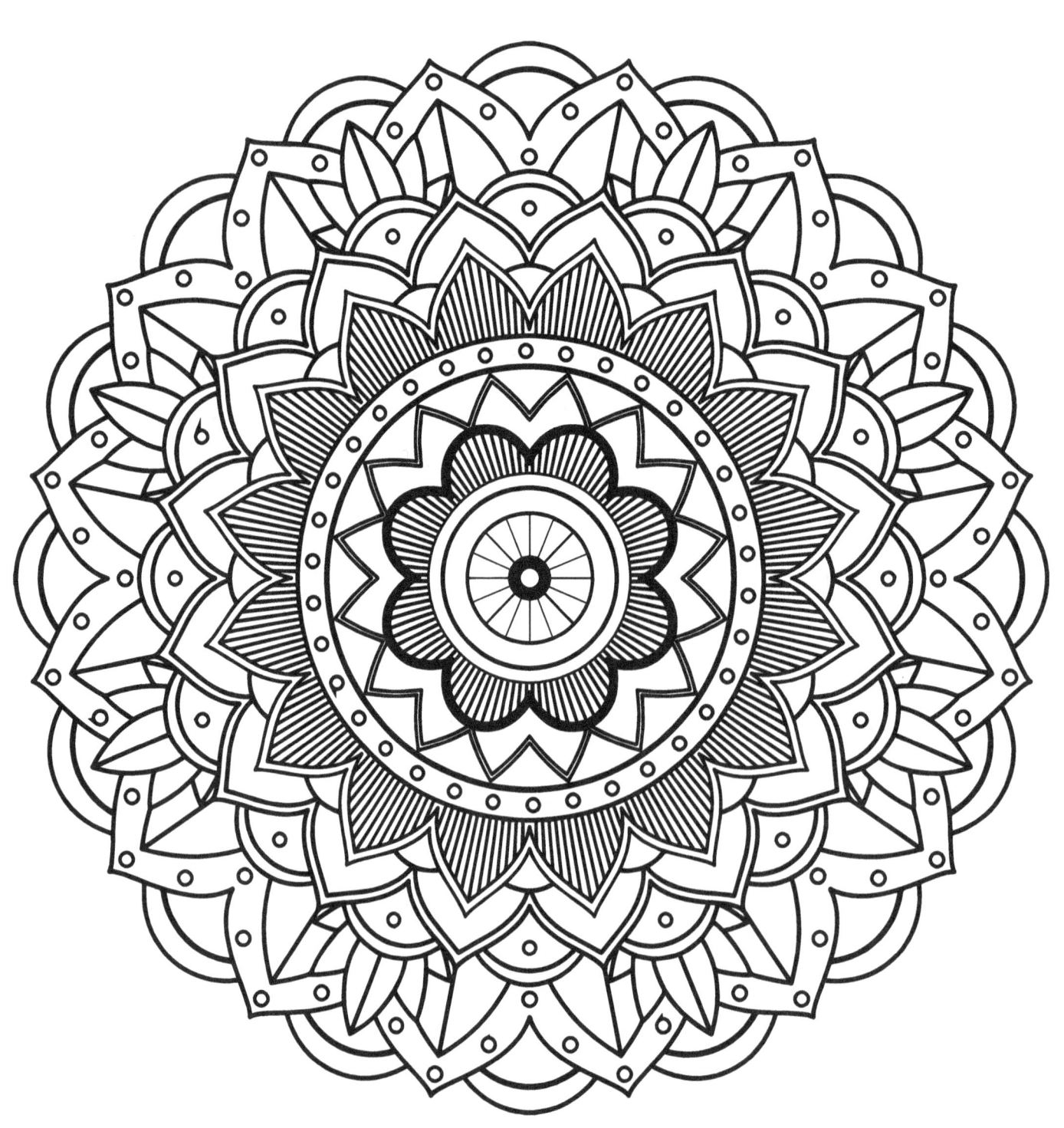

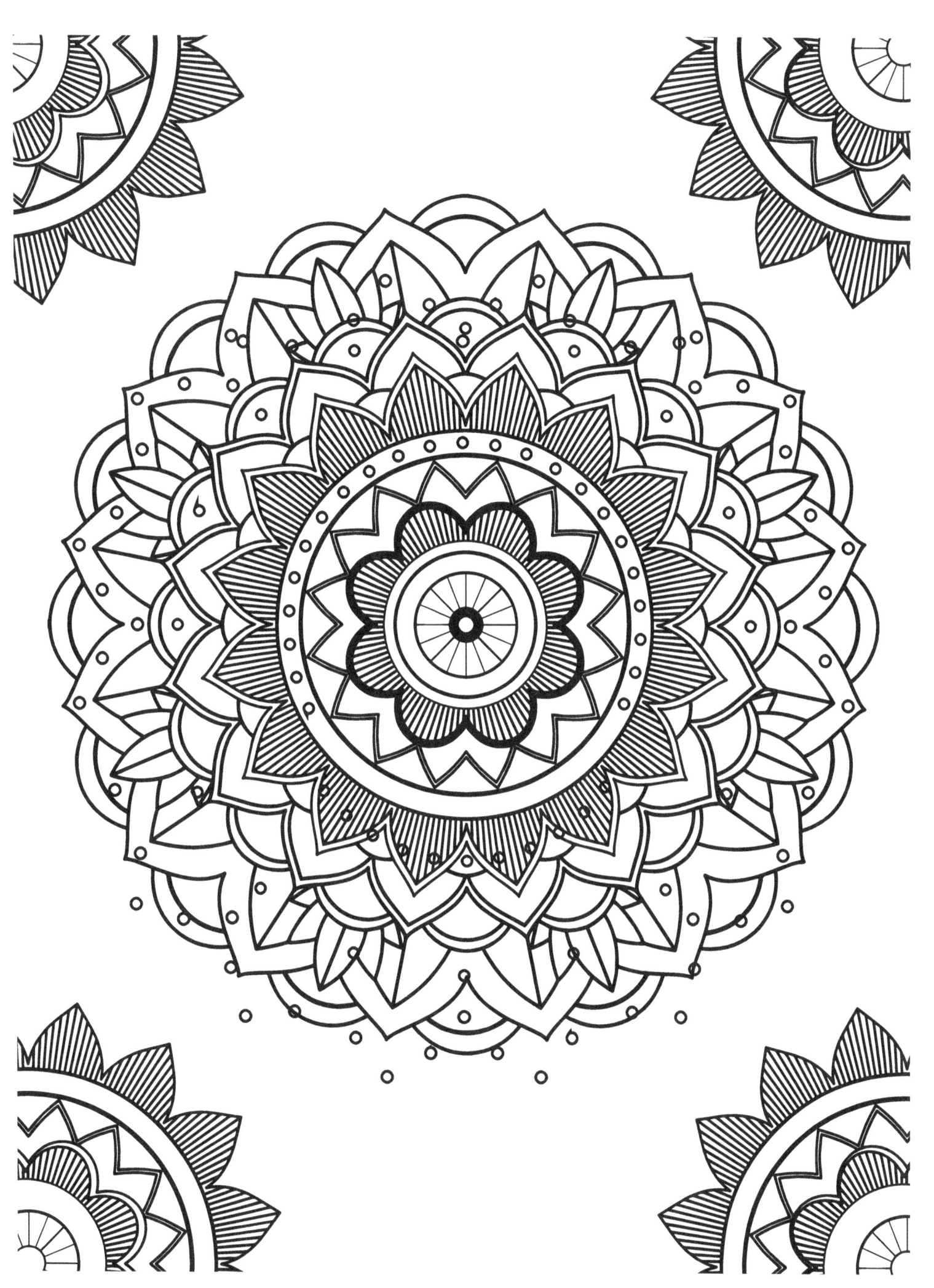

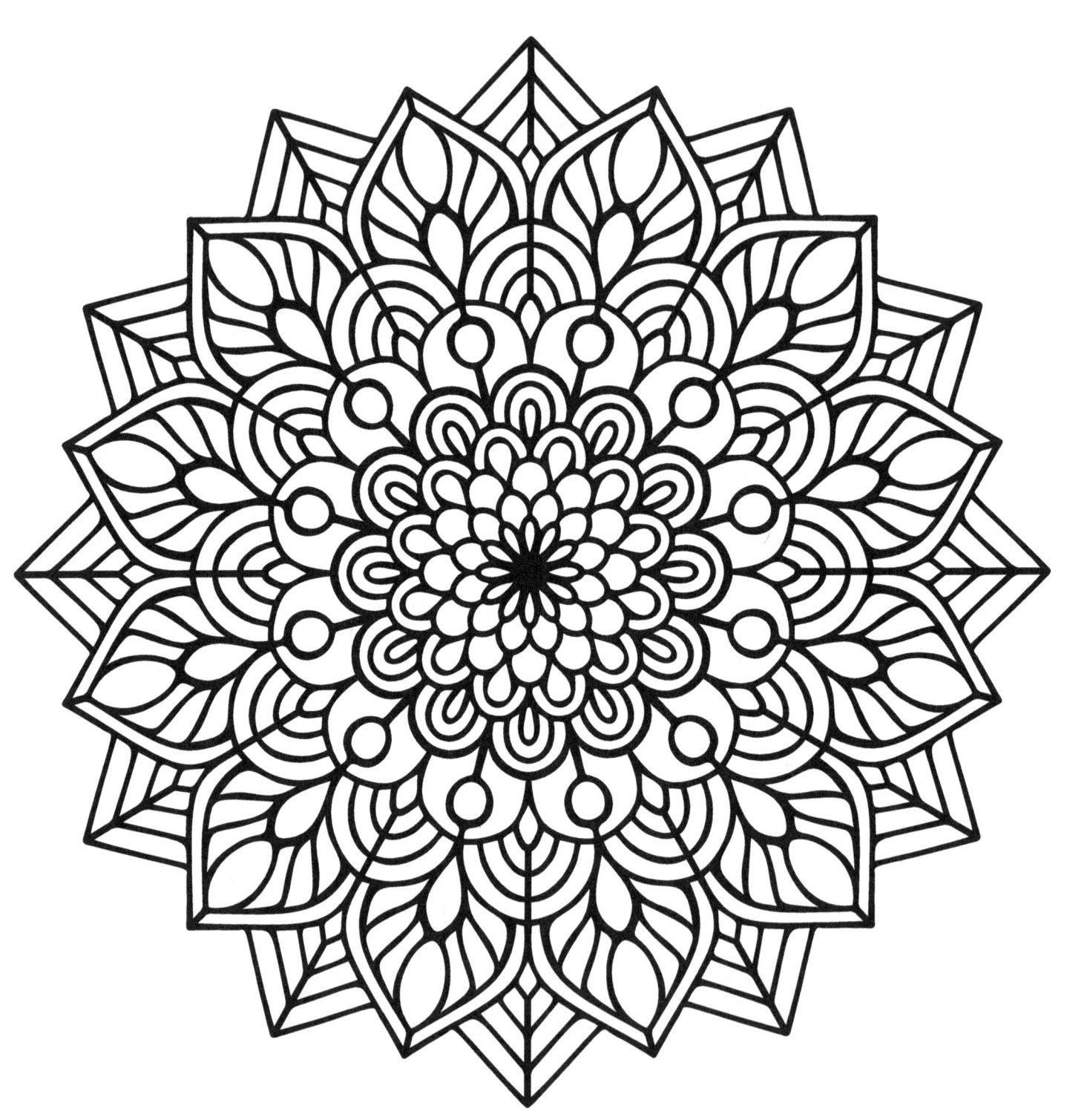

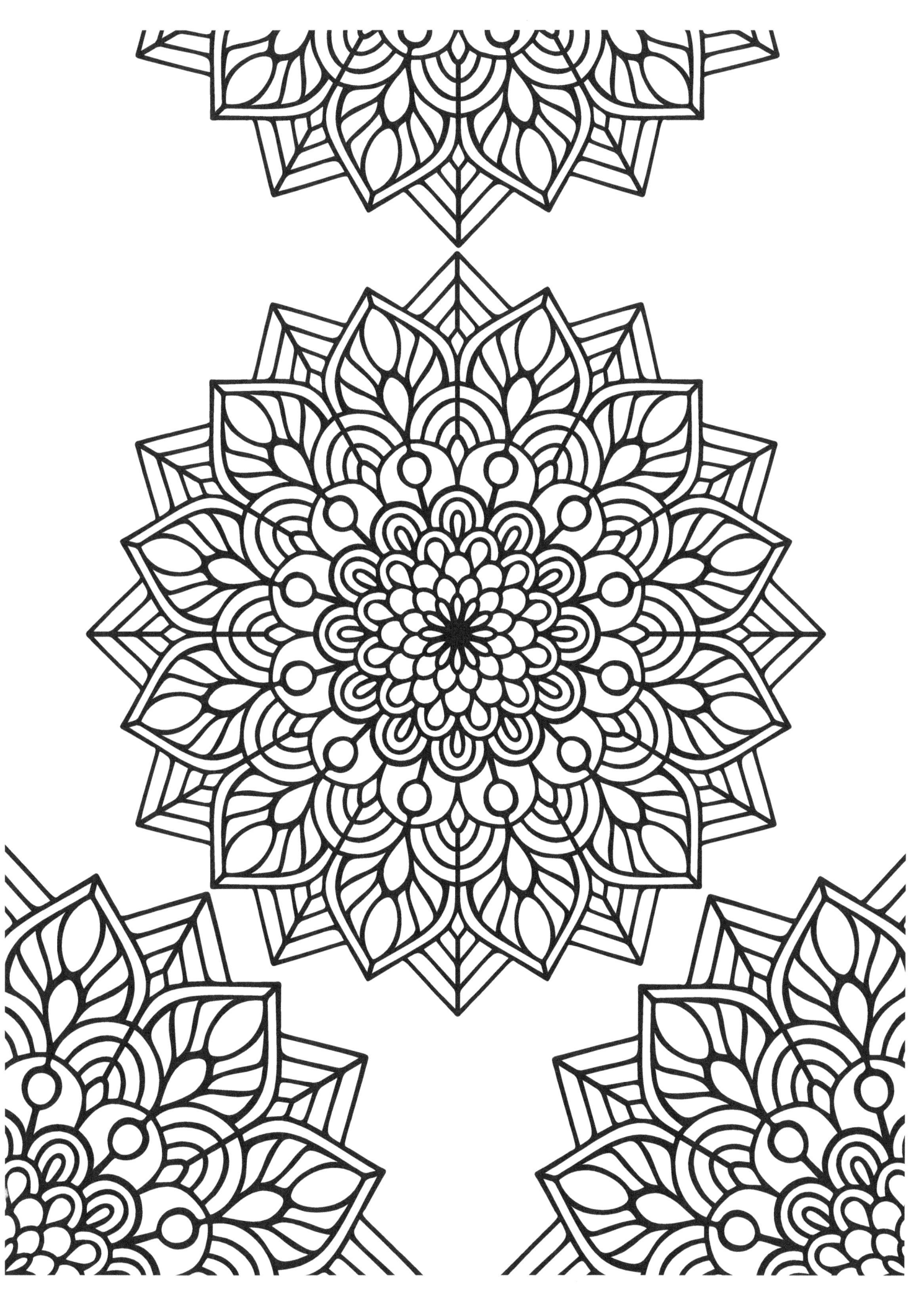

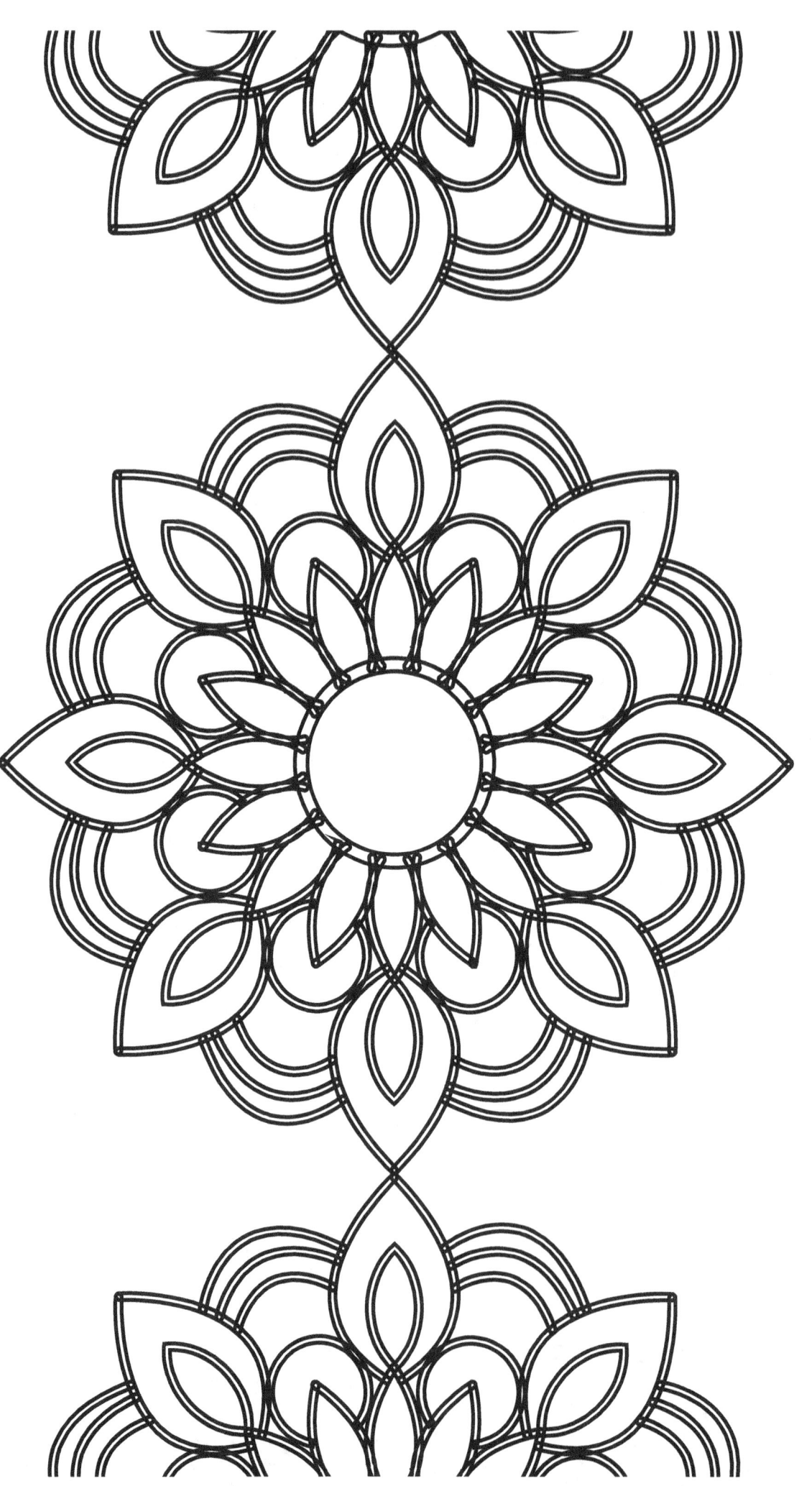

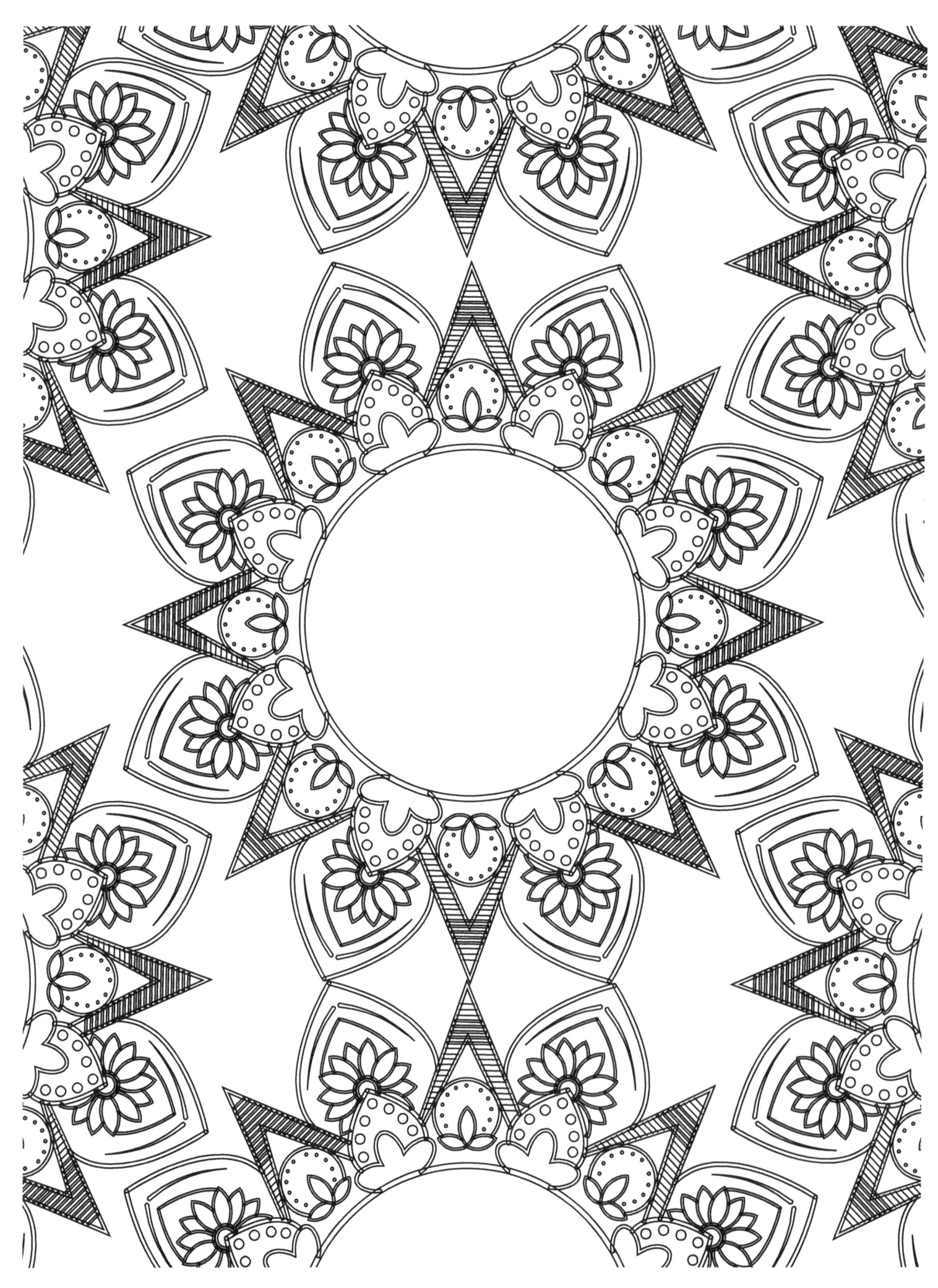

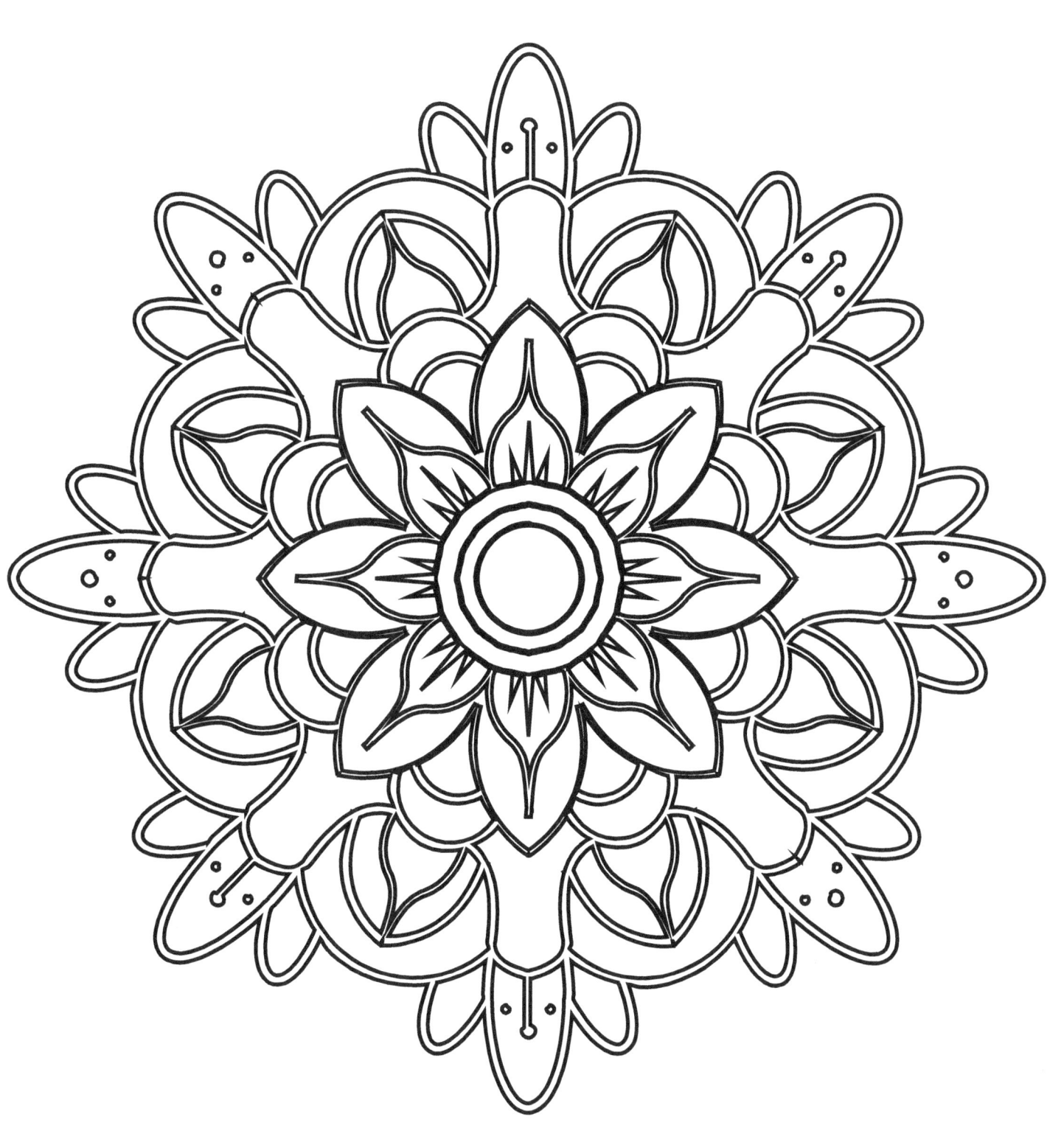

www.ingramcontent.com/pod-product-compliance
Lightning Source LLC
Chambersburg PA
CBHW081438220526
45466CB00008B/2436